Haunted San Diego

*A Historic Guide
To San Diego's
Favorite Haunts*

*Written and illustrated
by Gail White*

Tecolote Publications

© by Gail White. All rights reserved.

ISBN 0-938711-18-0

Library of Congress Cataloging Number 92-63385

First printing, December 1992.
Second printing, June 1993.
Third printing, March 1995.
Fourth printing, August 1996.

Tecolote Publications

San Diego, California

Printed in the United States of America.

Acknowledgments

This book would not have been possible without the rich sources of research available in San Diego. The vertical files on each subject matter at the San Diego Historical Society, the helpful people at the Escondido Historical Society, and the ever-popular California Room at the City Library.

The friendly staff at the Public Relations Departments of the Horton Grand and Hotel del Coronado were invaluable.

And most of all, a special thanks to my husband who often joined me on my treks to these most unusual places. Our experiences will make some great stories for the grandkids!

Sources

Bardacke, Frances, "The True Story of Yankee Jim,"
  San Diego Magazine.

Carrico, Richard L., *Ghosts and Hauntings in America's
  Southwest Corner.* Recuerdo Press, 1991.

Diary from Room 309, Horton Grand Hotel.

Elfin Forest Greeters, Elfin Forest, "The Whole Story."

Engstrand, Iris W., *Serra's San Diego.*
  San Diego Historical Society, 1992.

Escondido Historical Society, Vertical File on Harmony
  Grove.

Holzer, Hans, *Ghosts of the Golden West,*
  Ace Books: New York, 1968.

Lockwood, Herbert, *Fallout from the Skeleton's Closet,*
  Bailey & Associates, 1973.

May, Antoinette, *Haunted Houses of California.*
  California Living Book, 1977.

O'Connell, Mary Margaret, "Legends of Vallecitos."

Old Town San Diego State Historical Park, "Tour Guide and
  Brief History," Boosters of Old Town, 1988.

Rice, Edna Taft, *A Clairvoyant Approach to Hauntings,*
  California Parapsychology Foundation, Inc., 1968.

San Diego Historical Society, Vertical Files on each subject.

Table of Contents

Haunted San Diego

Haunted San Diego

Are there haunted houses and areas in San Diego County? Many long-time residents say that there are. While some people may make light of the idea of ghosts, many have had experiences that are hard to explain in any logical manner.

Most tourists come to San Diego for world famous animal parks, beautiful beaches, and first rate restaurants. Some get a little more than they had planned for. More than a few people have checked out of certain hotels in a hurry because a room for two suddenly became overcrowded. And countless people visited the Whaley House to find long-departed family members checking on their residence. For whatever reason, San Diego boasts a number of ghostly inhabitants who seem to love this city as much as the rest of us.

Not all of the haunted places are tourist attractions. Some are just innocent looking places such as Harmony Grove in North County. But many of the people who live in the area can tell you it loses much of its innocence when the lady in white decides to take a stroll in the moonlight.

This book can be used to get some background on the haunted areas, as most of them are historic places. It can be read with tongue in cheek if you're a bit skeptical. You won't be for long. Or better yet, use it as a guide book and go visit these places for yourself. All are open to the public and are great places to get a taste of why people say San Diego is one of America's finest cities.

What's the matter? You're not afraid of ghosts, are you?

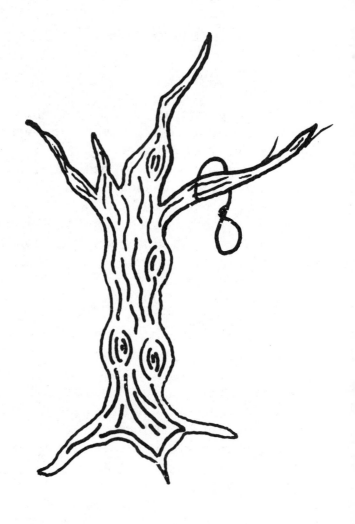

The Whaley House

The Whaley House
You can hang a good man, but he'll still hang around.

The year was 1852. Yankee Jim Robinson stood on a crudely structured scaffold with a noose around his large neck. The rope was tied to the mighty tree above and the mules were hitched up to the wagon. There was a large crowd of onlookers waiting to witness this grim event. Never believing he would soon be put to death, he began to address the audience about the injustices that had been dealt to him.

Yankee Jim was a notorious character from the Northern California gold fields. He had been found guilty of stealing San Diego's only pilot boat, the Plutus. While the boat was worth $6500, a very large amount for the time, a death sentence for an unscheduled boat ride does seem a bit excessive, especially when you consider that his two companions who were in on the heist with him only received a one year sentence.

There was a very strong feeling of vigilantism in pioneer towns in the mid-1800s. This was certainly true in the northern part of the state where Jim was from, and it was true in San Diego as well. The townspeople felt that the law had been too lenient in the sentencing of criminals and they were tired of it. There was great pressure on the local courts to deal harshly with the next individual to break the laws.

3

Unfortunately for Yankee Jim, a known desperado, he was that man. Fairness wasn't exactly a characteristic of the pioneer legal system. Upon capture, Jim had been severely wounded in the head. Although groggy and confused during the trial, he was heartily encouraged to represent himself. Emotion was running so high that there was an attempt by the townspeople to have him lynched right after the sentencing had been passed down rather than waiting the required thirty days. The angry crowd was talked out of it, however, and Jim was placed under supervision until September 18.

Jim talked to the audience up to the time of the hanging. After all, the people were just trying to teach him a lesson. Nobody really dies for stealing a pilot boat. Jim was right in the middle of a sentence when, silently, a motion was given to set the mules in action. Jim's neck was not broken instantly, putting him out of his misery. Instead, he slowly choked to death while the townspeople looked on. Forty-five agonizing minutes later, Yankee Jim Robinson was pronounced dead.

*   *   *

Among the onlookers on that fateful day was a San Francisco businessman named Thomas Whaley. Originally an eastern merchant, he had been lured to the west coast by the gold rush in Northern California. More interested in commerce than in mining, he set out on some very interesting business ventures dealing in hardware and mining equipment. Tragedy hit when a devastating fire consumed San Francisco and burned down the stores he had worked so hard to establish. When he was offered a partnership in a general store in San Diego, he jumped at the chance to relocate. The new business took off and prospered and he again found himself a very successful businessman. Whaley had promised himself that if he could make a success of his new enterprise, he would go back east and propose to his intended, Anna Lannay. The trip proved to be a triumph. Anna happily said yes to the all-important question and they were married in New York. Soon they were on their way back to San Diego to start their life together. Upon arrival, a ball was held in honor of the celebrated businessman and his new bride.

By the year 1856 they were the proud parents of two sons, Francis, and Thomas, Jr. Whaley felt the time was right to build a home for his growing family. He wanted this house to be the finest home in the entire area. He bought a lot in Old Town and even opened up a brick factory for the project.

When the house was completed, it was the envy of everyone for a hundred and fifty miles. Carpets from Brussels, rich rosewood and mahogany furniture, only the finest of everything. Both fond of music, the couple became known for their elegant musical soirees. Their first daughter, Anna, was born in this house and life seemed perfect for the young couple. They wanted for nothing.

Unfortunately, their happiness was short lived. Tragedy again struck in the form of a fire, destroying Whaley's store on the plaza. And little Thomas Whaley died at seventeen months in his upstairs bedroom. Grief-stricken, they felt they had to get away from San Diego. Leaving their business interests in the care of a trusted friend, they went back to San Francisco to be with friends and to try to put their terrible misfortunes behind them.

They were away from San Diego about ten years. During this time Thomas Whaley was appointed Commissary Storekeeper, U.S.A., and also went to Alaska to become a member of the Sitka city council.

By the time they were ready to return to San Diego, their family had grown to include three more children. Whaley quickly began to remodel his house to better accommodate his growing family. A new wing was added and the house was refurnished. Many balls and parties were held and the Whaleys were again the toast of the town.

Some rooms were leased out for public uses. T.W. Tanner and his wandering group of performers leased out an upstairs room, giving San Diego its first theatre. At various times parts of the house were used as a hotel, school, granary, saloon, jail, and even a dance hall.

In 1869 the city leased the north wing for $65.00 a month to be used as a courthouse. The county records were kept in some upper rooms. As time went on more and more people began to move to the San Diego area. Gradually the population began to shift from Old Town to "New Town." Public demand grew fierce to have the courthouse and public records moved to a more central location, but Old Town stood firm. Martial law was put into effect and a cannon was placed in front of the Whaley house. The San Diego *Union* boldly proclaimed, "Old Town Has Seceded!" and the situation looked grim. After a while, tensions lessened and Whaley felt it was safe to take a short business trip. Word of his absence got out and at midnight the enemy made their move. With greased wagons and gunny-sacked hoofed horses, the group silently crept into town. They broke into the house and held a terrified Anna Whaley at gunpoint on the ninth step of the stairs as they raided the courthouse.

When Thomas Whaley returned and found out about the incident he was enraged. Dozens of letters demanding reimbursement for damages as well as payment on the lease went unanswered. He finally had to let the matter drop.

The courthouse affair showed Thomas Whaley that the shift in population was a reality he would have to accept. He reluctantly put his house up for sale and moved his business ventures to New Town where he was to stay until his death in 1890.

The Whaley house did not sell and remained in the family. Corinne Lillian lived there until her death in 1953. The house was left to deteriorate and was scheduled for demolition when a group of concerned citizens came to its rescue in 1956. They formed the Historical Shrine Foundation and bought the land and the building. They later convinced the board of supervisors to turn the house into a museum. A committee was formed and furnishings were collected from other early pioneer families in a grand effort to restore the house to its glory years.

And that's when the fun began...

*   *   *

One thing for sure. You're never really alone at the Whaley House. Even before it opened to the public, strange things began to happen. June Reading, the director of the museum, heard footsteps upstairs one day when she was getting the place ready for opening. Thinking it was a delivery man, she went upstairs to investigate. No one was there. She went back down stairs but the footsteps persisted. Later it was discovered that the house had been built on the site where the infamous Yankee Jim Robinson had been hung one hundred years earlier. Yankee Jim never did believe he would die for his crime. It seems he still doesn't. While this was an eerie start for an historic museum, it was only the beginning.

Soon unexplained sounds began to be heard with remarkable frequency by museum workers and visitors alike. Many people have heard the anguished cries of a baby in the room where little Thomas Whaley died. A rich deep laugh can be heard echoing down the halls and music drifts through the house much as it did when the Whaleys entertained their friends.

It wasn't long before museum workers became accustomed to sounds as well as other unusual occurrences. Tired of having the upstairs windows pop open at all hours, four-inch bolts were installed to solve the problem. The windows still blew open, mostly in the middle of the night, setting off the burglar alarms. They became used to getting calls in the late night hours from the police notifying them of a breakin. Of course, when they arrived there was no evidence of any theft. Only open windows. The spirits apparently only wanted a little fresh air.

One guide decided to play the piano one night after the museum was closed. Sensing the presence of someone watching him, he turned to find a woman staring at him, dressed in clothes that were popular a century ago. Knowing of Anna Whaley's love of music, it is not hard to imagine how the melody prompted her to appear, then fade away before his eyes. Some workers reported seeing a small dog bathed in yellow light run down the hall, then disappear. Many have told of the aroma of bread and apple pie baking in the oven that has long ago stopped working. Anna Whaley's sweet perfume and Thomas Whaley's strong pipe tobacco can also be detected drifting through the house. Almost everyone senses the strange feeling at times of another presence in the room with them when they are alone.

Visitors are not in any way left out of the ghostly actvities. One peculiar thing about these spirits is that they don't seem to mind how many people are around or what time of day it is to go about their business. The image of the typical ghost roaming the halls at midnight with chains doesn't seem to apply here. That is not to say an encounter with one of the ghosts doesn't give the visitor something to write home about. One lady from Canada reported feeling a pressure as she went upstairs. It was as if someone, or something, didn't want her to go up there. She also felt cool breezes swirling over her head and a strong feeling that someone was behind her. Downstairs in the courthouse section, she saw a small dark woman in a long calico dress and hoop earrings. She got the distinct sensation she was intruding on the apparitions's privacy. When questioned about these unusual occurrences, the museum help didn't seem unduly alarmed. Just a typical day at the Whaley House!

A group of local school children were touring the house one day, happy to be there rather than in the classroom. Imagine their surprise when the heavy metal chains that separate the courtroom from the judge's bench began to swing back and forth without any apparent human help. Every school child there saw it with wide-eyed excitement. This was one field trip they would not soon forget. The courtroom is said to be one of the most haunted rooms in the house. Even when objects aren't moving around on their own, people say they feel uneasy and are unable to concentrate when in the area.

Children seem to be especially tuned in to certain areas of the house. Many relate seeing pots, pans, and other kitchen utensils move and clash around when in that part of the house. They also tell of hearing sounds of other children playing, laughing, and crying. History tells us that one of the Whaley children's playmates died in the kitchen after being brought there. She had been severely injured while playing outside. Her favorite room to play in while she was alive was the kitchen. It still is.

People also tell of an odd sensation on the ninth step of the stairway. We know this is where Anna Whaley was held at gunpoint during the break-in for the courthouse records. Some people remark that they have an unexplained feeling of pressure and fear when they reach that step. Maybe Anna Whaley is still traumatized by that horrible event back in the 1860s.

So many accounts of strange things were being reported that the directors of the museum thought that some outside help was in order. The California Parapsychology Foundation was called in to do a little psychic research on the place. Kay Sterner, president of the foundation and a known sensitive, agreed to make several visits to the house. It should be noted that she had no prior knowledge of the history of the house or the Whaley family. On her first visit, she preferred to stay outside and inspect the grounds. As she rounded the corner, she became aware of an ancient scaffold, with mules in the act of pulling away from it. It looks like our old friend Yankee Jim is still around. She peered up to an upstairs window to see a heavily made-up theatrical woman gazing out. No doubt a spirit from the Tanner Troupe hovering about, still looking to entertain the people of San Diego. She then saw a young woman wearing a mauve dress from another window. She later saw the same dress inside on one of the mannequins. It was hand made by one of the Whaley daughters, all of whom were excellent dressmakers.

On another visit she spent part of a night inside the house on the upper floor, alone while other members of the foundation and director June Reading waited downstairs. She became aware of a rugged large man in dark clothing and dusty boots. It was later confirmed that her description fit that of Thomas Whaley himself. She then saw a young woman walk slowly toward her carrying a razor with a whalebone handle. Kay Sterner had a strong awareness that the woman was consumed with thoughts of suicide. Afterward she learned that a young woman had indeed attempted to kill herself while staying at the house.

On another night at the house, Kay Sterner had a particularly frightening experience that left her pale and trembling. It was very dark in the house and she had to feel her way up the staircase. When she had reached the top, she began hearing agonizing screams. She then saw a Mexican couple having a violent argument about the woman being unfaithful to her husband. To the psychic's horror, the man took a knife and started stabbing his wife so violently he disemboweled her. She later learned that the couple had in fact been tenants of the house for a time and that a brutal murder had occurred.

A part-time guide became interested in the ghosts when he kept hearing the by-now famous footsteps. He received permission to spend a night in the house with a group of his friends from the Starlight Opera theater. A member of the parapsychology organization was there to supervise. The night? Friday the 13th.

The group was not disappointed. Chilly breezes churned overhead. A mysterious light appeared over a man's head, then drifted over to the portrait of Thomas Whaley. And, of course, heavy footsteps upstairs. If there were ever any non-believers in the group, they soon changed their minds.

They decided to break up into small groups. One of the groups witnessed a chandelier swing back and forth in one of the upstairs rooms. One individual felt an unseen presence touch him on the leg several times. In the study, a shadow appeared that was surrounded by a soft glowing light. In yet another room, the prisms on an antiqued lamp started moving on their own, all at different times.

They reconvened in the courthouse only to find even stranger things going on. They all placed their fingertips on the large heavy wood table and waited. After a while they heard a creaking noise as the table slowly shifted across the room a few inches. Then, to their amazement, it lifted off the ground on one corner where no one was touching it!

They decided to try a little mental telepathy to see if they could communicate with any of the spirits. Through a system of knocking known to psychic experts, they were able to "converse" with the ghost of a little seven-year-old red haired girl. She told them of other ghosts that reside in the house. The voice led them to the kitchen where the antique utensils began to swing around as she apparently started playing with them. Could this be the spirit of the little playmate of the Whaley children who died of her injuries in the kitchen?

Interest in the house reached a high pitch in the mid-1960s. Author and famed ghost buster Hans Holzer appeared on the Regis Philbin television show around this time to discuss a haunted house in San Diego. Our very own Whaley House! They became good friends and agreed to visit the house one day. The opportunity arose when Regis moved his talk show to San Diego. They decided it was time to confront the spirits.

They contacted well-known psychic Sybil Leek to help them and arranged to be at the house with a film crew the night of June 25, 1965. Although they tried to keep the event quiet, word got out and local excitement started to grow. Ghostly excitement grew as well. It is not unusual that when an investigation of this kind is about to take place, the spirits somehow sense the impending intruders and grow restless. The Whaley House ghosts are no different. About a month before the scheduled meeting, spirit activity picked up considerably. A tape recording of some music contained some human voices not heard when the tape was being made. Many times workers in the

house heard the front door open when there was no one there. One woman, as she was going upstairs, felt an icy wind hit her in the face with such force it made her hair stand up. Many people heard noises upstairs when the house was absent of tourists. They also reported feeling a strong presence close behind them as if someone were about to touch them. This usually occurred as they were getting ready to lock up. One volunteer distinctly saw an apparition appear in the form of a large man in a frock coat standing at the top of the stairs. The description fit Thomas Whaley exactly. One woman grew pale at the sight of a rocking chair rocking on its own. On a tour of the house, a woman felt herself being physically pushed out of one of the bedrooms by an unseen force. There was no doubt about it, the ghosts were ready.

Sybil Leek entered the house first to get an impression of the place while the others tried to discourage a small group of local people that had gathered in front of the house. When Hans, Regis, a small camera crew, and June Reading entered, Sybil told them she was sure there were several ghosts in the house. She had been drawn to the kitchen to see a little girl standing there. No little girl had been brought to the meeting. The impression of the little girl was especially strong. She was aware of much confusion and some hostility that exists within these walls.

A seance was quickly arranged in the courtroom with a motion picture camera running to record the events. During her trance, different voices erupted from her throat. They found out that the little girl's name was Anna Bell and that she died suddenly at the age of thirteen. She was confused and didn't seem to understand anything going on around her. Another voice took over and spoke of fever...every one having the fever. Then a more hostile entity began to communicate with Sybil. It was the spirit of a man. He spoke of official papers, injustices dealt to him, and wanting revenge from city officals. The spirit was angry. Too many people roaming around...HIS... house! Was this Thomas Whaley himself communicating with the visitors? It would seem that it was.

The party left early the next morning completely convinced the house is indeed haunted. When Regis checked back with June Reading a week later, he was informed it was business as usual...furniture rocking, chandeliers swinging, and footsteps pounding. This was one house Regis Philbin will never forget!

One summer a historical play was held at the house. It revolved around a trial and execution of an infamous ruffian who had stolen a pilot boat from San Diego Bay in 1852. Our very own Yankee Jim Robinson! It didn't take long for the fun to start. Soon after production started, many of the actors began to complain of an eerie feeling of being followed. The actress that played Anna Whaley was in the kitchen one day when she felt a hand run through her hair. When she turned around, no one was there. When an apparition appears it is common for a temperature change to take place. Just before she felt the touch, the kitchen had grown extremely cold. The actress was convinced she had contact with the spirit of the woman she was portraying.

Later a chair used by Thomas Whaley sometimes developed a soft mist around it. Unexplained shadows were seen by the actors and cigar smoke could be detected when the house was opened in the mornings. Some of the cast members heard the sound of a small child crying in the upstairs bedroom. And the footsteps...they occurred at an alarming rate. Perhaps it was Yankee Jim himself, pacing back and forth hoping this time, in the play, justice would be served and his life would be spared.

*   *   *

When Disneyland created its attraction, The Haunted House, they went straight to the experts—the people of the Whaley House. Through the years this house has become known as one of the most actively haunted houses in the country. It is even listed as one of the thirty ghost houses in this country by the U.S. Department of Congress.

When you visit the Whaley House, you will see many things. It is a fine museum. There are beautiful antique furnishings, quaint clothing, and examples of life as it was in the early days of San Diego. And, oh yes, it is quite possible you will see a ghost!

The Whaley House
2482 San Diego Avenue, Old Town
10:00 a.m. to 4:30 p.m. Seven days a week.
Times and days subject to change.
See map, page 17.

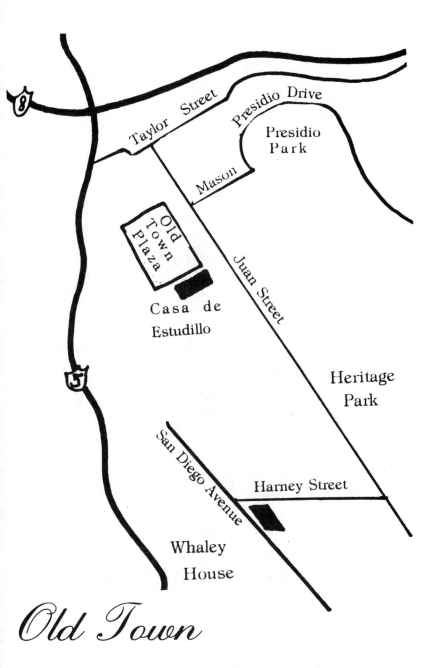

Old Town

Hotel del Coronado

Hotel Del Coronado

Kate Morgan checked in, but she never checked out.

The beautiful young woman looked pale and frightened as she checked into the exquisite Hotel Del Coronado. It was blustery and cold, only a few days before Thanksgiving, in the year 1892. She got her room and waited. And waited. She called the bellboy to have him bring her some wine to warm the coldness within her. Still no one came. She then realized what she had to do. There was a new life growing within her that would never have a future. After days of agonizing soul searching, she painfully aborted her unborn child. She then committed the ultimate escape. She went out to the veranda overlooking the gray ocean, put a revolver to her temple, and pulled the trigger. The newspapers referred to her as "The Beautiful Stranger."

*　　　*　　　*

A remarkable sight awaits visitors and locals alike as they cross the majestic bridge into the island community of Coronado. Off in the distance with the sparkling blue ocean as a backdrop stands one of the largest wooden buildings in the United States, The Hotel Del Coronado. The most striking feature of this historic building, however, is not its immense size, but the fairy tale-like quality of its architecture. The giant red-tiled roof sets atop the snow-white walls like frosting on a huge Victorian wedding cake. The many small-gabled windows peek out as if they were tiny sentinels keeping watch over the beautiful grounds. Lush lawns and exotic trees surround the building, giving it the quality of only the the finest resorts. Every aspect of the celebrated landmark echoes the romance of its exciting past.

The idea for the luxury hotel was born on a wintry day in February of 1886. Elisha S. Babcock and H.L. Story were out on a rabbit hunting expedition when it occurred to them that the locale would be an ideal location for a resort hotel. The timing was right on target as well. In the 1880s San Diego was in the middle of its "boom" years. The city was promoting its ideal climate to entice rich people from the east and midwest to leave their freezing environment for the sunny west coast. Since both Babcock and Story were from the east, they knew from experience that this tactic was a sure winner. Their early advertisements promised an "environment free from malaria, hay fever, mad dogs, cyclones, or cold snaps."

Plans were made, ground was broken, and the grand hotel opened for business in February of 1888. The elaborate advertising campaign paid off, for from the beginning the hotel was flooded with visitors. Not only did the resort attract affluent people from the east and midwest, as its reputation grew it attracted the famous as well.

Presidents were not strangers to the giant wooden masterpiece. Early visitors included the likes of Benjamin Harrison, William McKinley, Howard Taft, and F.D.R. Other notable early guests included Henry Ford and Montgomery Ward. Thomas Edison is even said to have helped with the wiring of the entire building as well as turning the switch to light the hotel's first Christmas tree. The early years also attracted such American aristocracy as the Astor and Vanderbilt families. Charles Lindbergh was once honored there with a gala dinner.

The atmosphere of the place fired the imagination of the literary set. Henry James came there for inspiration. L. Frank Baum, author of *The Wizard of Oz*, was a frequent visitor. Could it be that the fairy tale look of his castle in the land of Oz was influenced by the Hotel Del?

It wasn't long before the hotel became a playground for the Hollywood set. Hollywood's glamour years of the 1920s and 30s produced many movie stars that liked to vacation at the Hotel Del. Sarah Bernhardt, Mary Pickford, Mae West, and Tallulah Bankhead all found the place enchanting. Charlie Chaplin liked to play polo there. And when she wanted to be alone, this is where Greta Garbo came to escape.

Hollywood found the hotel irresistible as a movie set. In 1927 it was used in the silent film, *The Flying Feet* and in 1935 it was featured in the musical, *Coronado*. But by far, the most famous movie to be produced there was the enormous hit, *Some Like It Hot* starring the likes of Tony Curtis, Jack Lemmon, and the legendary Marilyn Monroe. Employees at the time talked in awe of the sight of Monroe gracefully floating down the halls in her beautiful gowns and playing on the beach with her famous co-stars.

More currently, television has used the famed hotel in some of its T.V. series. Parts of "Rich Man, Poor Man," "Hart to Hart," and "Simon and Simon" were all filmed there. Television stars to frequent the resort include Jimmy Durante, the Lennon Sisters, Robert Taylor, Donna Reed, and Bob Newhart.

One of the most famous events in the history of

the hotel involves the Prince of Wales. An elaborate dinner was thrown in the prince's honor, and being one of the world's most eligible bachelors, countless people showed up to get a look at him. One of the people at the reception happened to be Wallis Warfield, a married housewife, who lived within blocks of the hotel. Sparks must have flown during that first meeting, for although they were not to meet again until almost fifteen years later, he could not forget her. Fate brought them together again years later when she moved to London to be with her husband who had business in England. This time, when they met "officially" he was no longer the Prince of Wales, but King Edward VIII. By this time she was Mrs. Earl Spencer, having divorced her first husband. A romance started between them that would shock the world. King Edward chose love over royalty, giving up his throne to marry the twice-divorced Wallis Spencer. They became the famed Duke and Duchess of Windsor. The Hotel Del named its best gourmet restaurant "The Prince of Wales" to honor the fateful meeting many years before of this fairy tale couple.

One hundred years of history had passed for ths celebrated landmark in 1988. One of the largest birthday parties in hotel records took place over a three-day time period. There was a celebrity tennis tournament and a harbor cruise. The ballrooms turned into theme areas. One was a thirties style dinner and drive-in, one was a twenties style speakeasy and one was a disco for the younger crowd. You could be a part of the 1988 time capsule. Tony Curtis and Jack Lemmon of *Some Like It Hot* were in attendance, but alas, the legendary Marilyn Monroe was no longer with us. A white tie affair and a tented circus rounded out the three-day extravaganza. The cost for the three-day affair? A mere $5000 per couple!

Today the hotel is still a retreat for the famous. A total of ten U.S. presidents have stayed there, the latest being Richard Nixon and Ronald Reagan. Both local people and tourists alike love to frequent the beautiful restaurants and stores on the premises. The hotel possesses an elegant charm that allows you to be transported back to a time when life was slower and beauty, refinement, and grace were things to be treasured.

Oh yes, it does have one more thing...It has a ghost...

* * *

Legends differ about the spirit that haunts the Hotel Del Coronado. One particularly juicy one involves the mistress of one of the employees of the Del. This man held a position of high authority, as well as great visibility. Rumor has it that it may have been manager and owner E.S. Babcock himself. In any case, the unfortunate mistress found herself with child and committed suicide while staying in room 502. The body disappeared. One version has the management disposing of the body in the area where the swimming pool is today. Anything to avoid a scandal. One account states that the young woman who died in that room was married to a sea captain.

The most recurring story, however, involves a Lottie A. Anderson Bernard, or as she was otherwise known, Kate Morgan. She and her husband Tom had a rather inspired con game going in the late 1800s. They would ride the trains, going from town to town posing as brother and sister. As Kate was a very beautiful young woman, she had no trouble attracting rich male suitors. Wanting to please her, they would enter into card games with her husband, posing as her brother, L.A. Bernard. Needless to say, they always lost their shirt in gambling with the expert risk taker. When the couple found out that young Kate was expecting a baby, Tom Morgan was less than pleased. This would no doubt put an end to their present way of life. They were on their way to Coronado late in November 1892 when Tom got off the train in Orange County, instructing Kate to go on without him. He told her he would join her in a day or two. She would never see him again.

Legend has it that she checked into room 502 as Lottie A. Bernard. She spent five lonely days, including Thanksgiving, waiting for her husband. Many hotel employees grew concerned about her. She appeared pale and vulnerable from the day she arrived.

In vain she went to some other hotels in San Diego to see if her "brother" had checked in, possibly with another woman. She grew more and more desperate as the days went by. Kate went to a store to buy what she felt was her only way out. A gun. The next day she was found on the steps leading to the beach, dressed elegantly in black. She was dead.

There have been many accounts of strange occurrences in room 3502, Kate's old 502, for many years. Reports range from a general feeling of uneasiness to out and out fear. Many long time employees have had first-hand encounters with the unknown. Lights have been known to flicker on and off in the room, and some say they feel an icy cold draft outside the door. One man reported seeing the curtains pull back as if an unseen presence was gazing outside the window. Perhaps poor Kate still waiting and looking for her husband to come for her? One employee who stayed over reported that the windows kept opening, the plumbing groaned and gurgled all night, and the bed shook.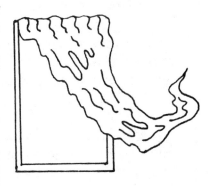

The housekeepers have a problem with the room as well. They will enter the room and do their jobs, only to return to find the soap, towels, and hangers rearranged for them. Some say the day, or night, they have to go into the room alone will be their last working at the hotel. One time a new young woman entered the room for the first time to do her housekeeping duties. She had no previous knowledge of the spirit that dwells there. First she just felt an eerie sensation, as though she were being watched. The strange feeling grew and intensified until she panicked and called her superior. The head housekeeper found her minutes later, still at the phone, so frozen in fear that she couldn't move. The shaken young woman had to be physically removed from the room. It was her first and last visit there. Most incidents are of a less frightening nature. One maid quietly tapped on the door and slipped a note under it inquiring if the occupants wanted their room straightened up. A slip of paper was returned with the message, "yes." When she entered, the room was empty! Kate has become so familiar with the staff, they even leave her an invitation to the annual Christmas party.

Many guests never last the night in that room. The reception desk is used to having people check out in the middle of the night in a grand hurry. Footsteps, water faucets turning by themselves, ice cold breezes on hot summer nights, are just a few of the reasons. Add to that strange moans and murmurs, windows that rattle, and a general feeling of uneasiness. Its no wonder people get a little uptight.

In May of the year 1983 one guest was in his room watching a little T.V. The news happened to be doing a feature on the hotel, and room 3502. With amusement, the guest realized this was the room he was staying in. He learned of the legend of Kate Morgan and the history of that infamous chamber. While the story interested him a great deal, he laughed it off as he did not under any circumstances believe in ghosts. He put the news story out of his mind and went to bed. After a while the chorus of gurgling pipes began. He thought it was strange, but told himself all old hotels made weird sounds. A little later, he awoke to a soft breeze and noticed the drapes gently billowing. Didn't they look ever so slightly like the skirts of a Victorian dress? He sighed and got up to close the windows. He found them securely locked. He was no longer laughing. Around midnight, a mysterious light enveloped the room in an eerie glow. Had to be the moon. He got up to find the sky covered in a thick cloud layer so common to the San Diego area in the spring. That was it! He hurried to the reception desk to request another room. He was told that because of all the stories surrounding the room, many people actually wanted to stay there. "Fine, let them have it!" was the reply. He was quickly moved to a less active part of the hotel. It turned out that this was not an average guest. He was one of then Vice-President George Bush's elite secret service guards, there to protect our future President. When word of his night of adventure got out he suffered merciless teasing

26

from the rest of the secret servicemen. He did, however, receive a special plaque for surviving at least part of a night in the infamous room, as well as a healthy respect for things that go bump in the night.

Until recently everyone took it for granted that the official haunted room was room 3502. This is no longer the case. Strange occurrences have been happening in another room as well. It might be wise to look at room 3312.

A man was resting on the bed in room 3312 one afternoon when he felt compelled to look at the television. Two feminine, beautiful eyes glowed on the screen along with a soft smile! As he looked on in

disbelief, the eyes glowed brighter. He ran to the hall to look for some moral support. When he returned with a bellman, the face on the screen was no longer smiling. As he moved around the room, the eyes sadly followed him. It was as if the spirit was sorry he had revealed her to another person.

One guest who knew of the legend of Kate Morgan was assigned to room 3312. On one of San Diego's glorious days, he decided to go for a walk on the grounds below his room. He glanced up and saw that all was quiet. He ran into a maintenance man who was replacing one of the lights at the end of the stairway. He complained that the light never stayed on for more than a day or two before it had to be replaced again. He wasn't aware that this was the site of Kate Morgan's demise, but the hotel guest was. The worker also said he constantly had to replace the screens on room 3312 above, as they kept falling off for no apparent reason. The woes of a mantenance man, he lamented. The guest nervously glanced up at his room to see the curtains gently waving in a breeze. He knew for a fact that the windows were closed.

Research shows that the hotel has undergone two major renovations in its history. Room numbers have greatly changed over the years. Old registers found at San Diego State University reveal that a Kate Morgan checked into room 302, now room 3312, in late November of 1892, not room 502, as previously believed.

Alan May, an attorney, did much research on the room 302 versus room 502 question. He shed a lot of light on the legend of the haunted rooms. But no clear-cut answers arose. He felt sorry for the wandering spirit and erected a gravestone on the previously unmarked resting spot of Kate Morgan at Mt. Hope Cemetery.

So—are both rooms, 3502, and 3312, possessed of spirits? Apparently they are. While Alan May's research clearly shows Kate Morgan stayed in room 3312, it still doesn't explain years of baffling events in room 3502. It was revealed that room 3502 belonged to a maid who stayed at the hotel at the time Kate was a guest. She grew fond of Kate in the short time she was there and was extremely distraught when Kate's body was found. After Kate killed herself, the maid was never heard from again.

While Kate is by far the most famous spirit residing at the hotel, she is not the only one to make herself known. Psychics called into investigate have uncovered a few more. One day in the 1950s, a little girl named Melissa was staying there with her aunt. She was playing out in the hall with her favorite doll when she took violently ill. In the rush to get her some medical help the doll was left behind. Melissa did not have the good fortune to recover from her illness, but her ghost did. She is often seen sadly roaming the hallways still looking for her beloved toy playmate. One of the psychics also came across a little girl and boy who playfully ran up and down the stairway between the second and third floors. The Crown Room's first caretaker can sometimes be seen roaming around tapping the floor with his cane the way he did when he was alive. Lastly, there is the vision of a beautiful woman in an elegant Victorian dress floating effortlessly across the dance floor.

*   *   *

Visiting the Hotel Del Coronado is a special occasion any time of the year not only for tourists but locals alike. In the spring the grounds are ablaze with the growth of new flowers and plants. There is a fresh newness in the air that is intoxicating. The summer brings its throngs of tourists who take full advantage of the perfect beach for swimming, surfing, and just enjoying the warmth of the sun and the gentle sea air. It's a more casual time of year, and the long nights are ideal for leisurely dining on the outdoor patios. In fall there is excitement in the air as the holiday season approaches. The theatre and opera season brings with it a more formal party-like atmosphere that precedes the glory of the magical season to come. At Christmas time, the Hotel Del shines its brightest. The ceiling-high Victorian Christmas tree is a vision of incredible beauty. The short cool nights prompt romantic dinners in the glorious Prince of Wales room. And the magnificent Crown Room plays host to a boy's choir that serenades diners with the carols of the season.

A trip over the bridge to this grand old hotel any time of year is special. But remember that behind the grandeur, the fame and glamour, there is a more somber side to this building. Be sure to stop by and pay your respects to Kate. And always keep one eye over your shoulder, for you never know when you will run into a guest that has been part of this scene for one hundred years.

Hotel Del Coronado
1500 Orange Avenue, Coronado.
See map, page 31

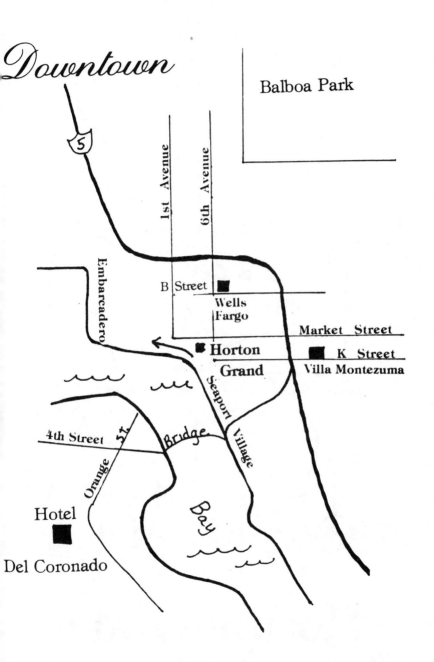

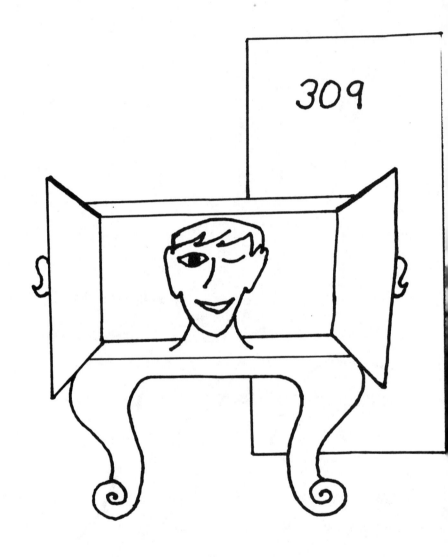

Horton Grand

The Horton Grand Hotel

Roger had a great poker face, but now it's lost its flush.

R oger A. Whittaker was much like the other men who used the gaslamp district as a hangout in the mid-1800s. A hard drinking, brash gambling man without a great deal of respect for the law. In his spare time he was a pimp. The gaslamp district of San Diego was a haven for Roger at this time in its young history. Drunken sailors, on leave after many months away from home, could be seen stumbling around, going into the numerous brothels that lined the streets. But this night Roger had no interest in joining the drunken group of ruffians. His gambling debts had finally caught up with him and there was a search party out for blood. His getting caught cheating didn't help matters much. He had already been shot once that fateful night, but he was able to make it back to his hotel. He hid out in an armoire in his room, fighting for his life. He felt safe, thinking they wouldn't look for him in a piece of furniture. He was wrong. Just as he thought he was out of danger, the armoire door opened and a giant thug of a man filled him with gun shot. Roger was at last out of the enormous gambling debts he had piled up for himself. Roger was dead.

*   *   *

The enchanting Horton Grand Hotel lies in the colorful Gaslamp District of San Diego. It is made up of two historic buildings, the Grand and the Kale

Saddlery hotels. Both have intriguing histories that make them an important part of San Diego's past. The Kale Saddlery is most famous for its association with Wyatt Earp. The west's most famous gunslinger arrived in San Diego in 1886 after his well known shoot-out at the O.K. Corral. The scene was right out of a classic western. Four good guys against four bad guys in the streets of Tombstone, Arizona. The good guys, dressed in black for a change, bravely approached the four outlaws. Within seconds, all chaos broke out and more than thirty shots were exchanged. When the dust cleared, two of the outlaws were dead and two had run away. Wyatt's partners were injured but still alive. The only one that was left standing through the whole ordeal was Wyatt Earp.

Wyatt was a gambler and prospector, fond of speculating in the real estate market. He heard about San Diego's "boom" years of the mid-1800s and decided to head west.

He checked into a hotel that at the time was named the Brooklyn. He felt right at home from the beginning, as the waiters in the restaurant had regular fist fights and shoot-outs. While he dabbled in a number of real estate ventures, his most successful outing came from the three gambling halls he operated. Wyatt did a fair amount of gambling himself. At one point he even won a race horse and proceeded to race it throughout most of the western states.

Sadly, the boom years were over as quickly as they started. Wyatt was able to keep his investments for five more years. When a depression hit the area, however, he sold out and moved north to another frontier, Alaska. The riches of the Klondike were calling his name. The hotel became the only reminder in San Diego of the colorful, exciting man that so represented the wild west.

From 1912, the bottom floor became home to the famed Kale saddle shop, the biggest maker of saddles in the west. Widely known for its beautiful leather work, it attracted the business of some of the biggest western stars. Roy Rogers, Leo Carrillo, Tom Mix, and Jackie Coogan were all regular customers.

By the late 1970s, time had caught up with the historic hotel and it was doomed by the city for destruction. Its glory days were over.

While the Saddlery was a fine example of what was called "cowboy Victorian" architecture, it was the Grand Hotel that stood out as the Victorian jewel of downtown San Diego. A German emigrant wanted to fashion the building after the opulent Innsbruck Hotel in Vienna. Great care was taken to see that every detail resulted in a work of art that was unique for the young city. Distinctive ornamentation, cantilevered balconies, and a split staircase carved from 100-yearold oak by the best artisans added up to a Victorian masterpiece.

Important people frequented the hotel. President Benjamin Harrison, Secretary of War Redfield and even David Kalakan, the president of Hawaii all found their way to the Grand Hotel. The hotel acquired its name of Horton Grand in 1907 in honor of the founder of "New Town," Alonzo Horton.

The most glamorous period of the hotel's life was in the mid-1930s when a lively vaudevillian named Bob Johnson operated the hotel. He ran the theatre next door and became well known for his burlesque reviews and colorful song and dance routines. Besides his association with the entertainment industry, he also had many contacts with the world of horse racing and boxing. The Palace sports bar at the

Horton Grand became the center of action for the elite set. Professional sports people and entertainers often frequented the place for talk and libation. George Jessel, funnyman Lou Costello, and boxer Joe Louis were all regulars. And there were always lots of celebrity seekers there to help round out the lively crowd.

By the middle of the sixties, the area teemed with strip and peep shows and began to show signs of decay. Johnson would not allow his girl performers to go to such extremes so he gave up his interest in the theatre and the hotel. The end of the burlesque era marked the end of the glamour days of the Horton Grand. It soon became just another rundown building in an even more rundown part of town.

In 1981 downtown San Diego experienced a transformation. There were plans underway for overhaul of the Gaslamp District and a clearing of land to make way for a shopping mall called Horton Plaza. Both of the old hotels were to be destroyed.

When word got out on the city's decision, the public was outraged. A group stepped in to try to save the hotels. They felt that relocation was the only answer. Both buildings were painstakingly taken apart piece by piece and stored in a warehouse until a proper site could be chosen for them.

The hotels were relocated in the newly revamped Gaslight District. This was an excellent choice on the part of the developers. This area's history is as colorful as any other in all of San Diego. It was here that the young city had its red light district. The Horton Grand was to sit on the site of Ida Bailey's establishment. Ida was San Diego's most famous madam, known for her quiet ladylike manner. She even had strict rules for her "girls." They had to behave in a dignified manner, couldn't smoke, drink, and wore little makeup.

To be sure, not all of the Gaslight District's activities were carried out with such refinement. The area was well known for its opium dens, gambling parlors, and rough drinking spots with names like "The Seven Buckets of Blood Saloon." The Chinese had a community there and were well known for having Chinese shoot-outs. It seemed appropriate to relocate these historic buildings to an area whose history so well represented a young rowdy frontier town.

The hotels were put back together again as they had been torn down, brick by brick. Great care was taken to see that the Victorian facade was preserved. Any and all usable artifacts were salvaged to guarantee the buildings were as authentic as possible. Craftsmen from Europe were brought in to restore the split oak staircase. When the project was completed, San Diego truly had a Victorian masterpiece in its midst.

Today they stand together joined by a New Orleans-type atrium. History and elegance are everywhere. Staff are dressed in period costumes. Their gourmet restaurant is named after the glamorous Ida Bailey. No two rooms are alike. Each has different antique furnishings and armoires are used instead of closets. They pride themselves on the fact that every room is different. Oh yes, one room is especially different. It is haunted...

*   *   *

Every room at the Horton Grand has a diary. Guests are encouraged to tell of their impressions of San Diego as well as their activities while here on vacation. The diaries are full of the accounts of fun-filled days at the beach, encounters with the animals at the zoo, and romantic nights on the town written by love-struck honeymooners. However, there is one exception. The diary in room 309 is filled with references to Roger, the playful ghost that haunts that beautiful room.

From the day the hotel opened for business in June of 1986, people knew there was something different about the room. Some maids refused to enter, and those who did usually wished they hadn't. They told tales of the beds shaking, lights turning on and off by themselves, and a general uneasy feeling of being watched. The few maids who weren't afraid to enter the room sometimes couldn't get in because the room had been deadbolted from the inside, even though the room was empty. When they did get in, they usually found something amiss. The soap had been misplaced, lamps were placed on the bed, and once the curtains were found tied in knots. Sometimes a distinct outline of a man's body can be seen making an indentation on the bed, when no one had been let into the room. One brave young chambermaid would enter the room, but only after she annouced her presence to Roger first. After some shaken guests began checking out in the middle of the night, management decided to look into the matter. They invited two psychics to spend the night in the haunted room and see if they could get some information on their unusual guest. They were not disappointed. All was quiet in room 309 upon arrival. The psychics credit this fact to the large group of reporters and cameramen who showed up to record the event. Ghosts are extremely camera shy. After the excitement of the media attention died down, however, the ghost gave the psychics quite a show.

Through mental telepathy they learned that the spirit was that of a Roger A. Whittaker who was shot in a gambling episode in the mid-1800s. He told them he died in another room at another hotel that is no longer here. But he stays in room 309 because it reminds him so much of his old room, and he feels at home there. Even the armoire is like the one he unsuccessfully hid in on that fateful night. Could this be the reason so many guests report the armoire doors opening and closing on their own at all hours of the night?

Roger seemed to enjoy his psychic visitors. When they played some music for him, they felt swirling drafts above their heads as if he were dancing on the ceiling. He also entertained them by turning the lights on and off and playing with the pictures. The psychic's opinions about Roger? "I think he's fun," one of them concluded.

As word of the haunted room spread, Roger's popularity grew. At times it is impossible to get reservations confirmed for room 309 as more and more brave souls want to experience Roger for themselves.

The diary is the most compelling piece of evidence of Roger's existence. He doesn't make his presence known to every guest, but he does to many.

Roger has been known to have physical contact with some people. It's not hard to imagine why one person complained that it was hard to go back to sleep when she was awakened by an icy hand on her shoulder. She was alone in the room at the time. One person awoke one night because she felt someone pulling on her arm. When she opened her eyes, there was a strange mist at the foot of the bed. Another young lady wrote of feeling something brush against her back for at least two minutes while she was sitting on the bed. A startled lady felt two cold arms suddenly go about her shoulders almost like a ghostly hug. Could it be possible that ghosts are in need of affection too?

A great number of guests reported on Roger's very annoying habit. It's his obsession with heat. Countless nights have been interrupted by a dramatic rise in room temperature. When the guests are awakened by the stifling heat, they run for the airconditioner, only to find it already set as low as 65 degrees. Even opening the windows doesn't help. One good-natured woman commented that she really didn't mind the heat at all. Her husband always kept the bedroom too cold anyway.

We learn from the diary that Roger has no desire to give up his gambling habit. He kept one couple up most of the night with the sounds of a ghostly poker game. They could hear the cards being dealt as well as the silver being dropped on the betting table. They don't know if he won, but at this point of the game it probably doesn't matter anymore. One couple was playing cards when they decided to go out for dinner. They remember leaving the cards stacked in a neat pile on the bed. When they returned there were two hands of cards laid out. One was a full house! Another card playing couple never could find the deck of cards they left on the counter, the only card left was the King of Hearts.

Roger likes to show his playful side to some of the guests that stay in his room. People constantly return to find the pictures turned upside down. One very old picture of a woman is sometimes turned with her face to the wall. The word "VAMP" is written on the back, and much speculation has taken place as to who the woman is. Staff and some guests seem to think that possibly Roger thinks she was a vampire and is just too scary for him. Some people try to test Roger. One man put a coin under a glass and one in a matchbook, and left them on the mantle. Upon his arrival, everything looked as it had when he left, except the coin under the glass had been moved into the bathroom. Just for fun, one couple left a nightcap of champagne for Roger in the armoire. When they awoke in the morning, they laughed and decided to share the drink before going downstairs for brunch. Roger had beat them to it, the champagne was gone. Upon arriving back to their room, a couple found that the beds had been mussed, "Vamp" had been turned around, and a vase of flowers had been placed between the  beds. For a finishing touch, the husband's sunglasses had been placed atop the only lamp left on. It's good to see Roger hasn't lost his sense of humor.

While Roger has the higher profile, it appears that he may not be the only spirit that lurks around this historic hotel. Heavy footsteps can be heard in many of the other rooms. In fact, while staying in Roger's room, many people have complained of all the traffic in the room above them. When they checked out the next morning, they were informed that the room was vacant all night. Since all the employees dress in period costumes, one guest wasn't surprised to see a man walking around on the third floor dressed in western garb. That is, until he disappeared before his eyes! Local people attribute all this ghostly activity to the bawdy history of the Gaslamp District. Considering all the saloons, opium dens, brothels, and gambling parlors that were in the area it isn't surprising that there are a large number of restless souls hovering around. It's no wonder Roger finds the hotel so much to his liking.

The Horton Grand Hotel is truly one of a kind. To visit it is to go back in time and become part of the mid-1800s. The elegant Palace Bar is the perfect place to go for a quiet afternoon break. Afternoon "high tea" rivals the best in London. The beautiful Ida Bailey's restaurant serves superb traditional American dishes. You can even see Ida herself if you drop by the concierge desk. The young lady that works there is costumed just like the elegant madam so many years ago. And if you decide to spend a night or two in this historic building, be sure to request room 309. Roger would just love to see you.

Horton Grand Hotel
311 Island Avenue, corner of Fourth
Downtown San Diego.
See map, page 31.

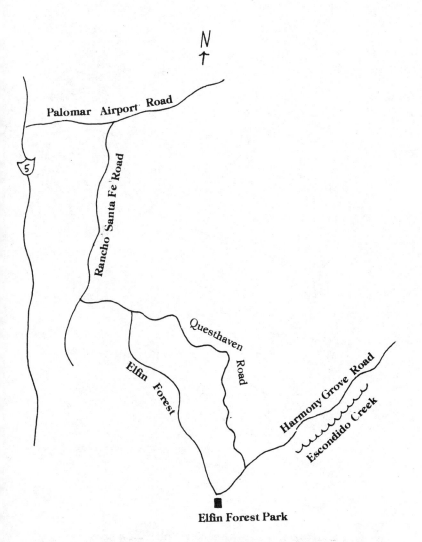

N

Palomar Airport Road

5

Rancho Santa Fe Road

Questhaven Road

Elfin Forest

Harmony Grove Road

Escondido Creek

■ Elfin Forest Park

North County

Harmony Grove

Harmony Grove
A Ghostly Sight: The Lady in White, riding her horse in the pale moonlight.

The night was perfect for an old-fashioned hay ride. The air was fresh and clear and everyone was in the mood for a party. It was Halloween.

Little white "spooks" lit up the driveway to one of the beautiful homes in the area. The hosts were giving a costume party to benefit a local charity and everyone was encouraged to come dressed as his or her favorite Halloween ghoul. No one was disappointed. Every monster from Dracula to Frankenstein was well represented. The apple cider flowed freely and the colors of black and orange were everywhere. Although it was the 1980s, the celebration retained a down-home, folksy quality that reminded everyone of a simpler way of life.

As the horse-drawn carriages piled high with freshly cut hay pulled out into the starlit night, many people felt a rush of anticipation. After all it was Halloween and one never knew what to look for in this area. Many locals claim that this part of the north county is haunted. As the carriages slowly made their way through the gently winding roads, it became clear that this was no ordinary hay ride. Pairs of piercing red eyes began to peek through the lush plant life that lines Harmony Grove. Images of ghosts could be seen hovering in the distance. A headless horseman startled everyone as he sped past the carriages. The night air was filled with the sounds of chains rattling and low mournful moaning.

As the carriages rounded the last bend of the trip, the most bizarre image of all greeted the astounded crowd. Bathed in a misty light, a young woman sat atop a beautiful white horse. The folds of her dress billowed out around her in a gentle breeze. She was dressed entirely in white. As the carriages drew nearer, the horse turned to walk away slowly and disappeared in the distance, much to the amazement of the crowd of onlookers.

When the guests returned, they heartily congratulated their hosts for making this a most remarkable Halloween. They thought all the special effects of the hay ride were spectacular. But when the lady in white was mentioned, the hosts looked surprised and confused. The pre-planned ghosts and sounds they were well aware of, but a lady in white was not part of the program. It was a somewhat shaken crowd that left the party that fateful Halloween night. For many of them realized that they had come face to face with Harmony Grove's mysterious Lady in White.

*   *   *

Harmony Grove's past is bathed in a magical quality. Many ancient Indian tribes considered the area to be a mystical place with a beneficial aura. The Northern San Dieguéno Indians were some of the first to arrive here from the east. Legend tells us they were led to the area in care of the gentle "Wind Spirit." Evidence suggests that Indian tribes could have been here as long as 9,000 years ago. They left behind a collection of metates, pictographs, and mortars. They also left a petroglyph, a kind of direction finder along the lines of those found in Stonehenge, England, although a smaller version.

The chaparral that grows in the area makes it undesirable for pastureland. Because of this, the land wasn't a major factor in the Mexican and Spanish land grants of the mid-1800s. However, Harmony Grove's claim to fame came with the Spiritualists' group that moved to the area in the late 1800s. The Harmony Grove Spiritualist Association was formed to promote a religion that firmly believes the soul survives the event of death. They also believe that spirits can communicate.

They started out as a small peaceful group, their homes dotting the gently winding road. As interest grew in the association, they decided to organize a summer festival to promote the ideas of their philosophy. These summer "camps" proved to be an enormous success. There were cabins and sleeping rooms and a communal dining room built to accommodate the guests. They spent the summer meditating, conducting seances and faith healing sessions. Speakers were invited to give talks on trances, clairvoyance, and the use of mediums in their religion. They also entertained their guests with more traditional pastimes, such as music and dancing. The camp usually ended with a grand "all mediums" day.

These summer camps were so popular in the forties and fifties that they attracted hundreds of followers. They also helped to earn the area the nickname of "Spooks" canyon.

Gradually interest faded in the activities of the Spiritualist group and the crowds stopped coming. Today the festivals are but a fond memory for the psychics that still live in Harmony Grove and practice their teaching.

In 1959 two prominent businessmen purchased twenty acres of land to be used as a vacation campland,

and Elfin Forest was born. The location was not far from the original Spiritualists' site. A manmade lake was made and spaces were provided for trailers and mobile homes. A tiny store was constructed to allow campers to drop in for the necessities: hot dogs, beer, soda, and pork and beans. Once again the area was filled with happy campers. Only now boat rides, movies, and square dancing replaced the stranger endeavors of the Spiritualists.

Eventually the land was sold and campers were no longer encouraged to use the property for vacation purposes. However, the small store and the whimsical entrance still remain.

Today Harmony Grove is an affluent area of upscale homes. Truly a rural spot, without a shopping mall in sight. In the last few years, a strong sense of community spirit has sprung up among the townspeople. They formed a town council and planned many local events, such as a Fourth of July parade and picnic and a lively Christmas light competition. The area is beautiful any time of year for a Sunday drive, to stop along the creek and dangle your toes in the clear water. You can stop by Elfin Forest's little store for refreshments. But be warned. If this is attempted on a misty twilight evening, there's every chance you will be approached by a mysterious "Lady in White"...

*   *   *

It's known as the Elfin Forest Cruise. A group of teenagers will pile into their car on a warm summer night and roam the winding streets of the Harmony Grove area. They are searching for an occurrence that has captured the imaginations of residents for years.

48

Many times they are rewarded with a sighting of the Lady Bathed in White.

Legends vary as to why the spirit haunts this beautiful valley. One version has a young woman coming to the area from the east. Her husband and son had come to California to look for land and had been killed by Indians. The young widow was devastated and refused to accept the fact she was now alone. Only if she could find their graves would she admit the tragedy had occurred. She came out west and mournfully roamed the valley in search for her loved ones' graves., The house she was staying in caught fire, trapping her inside and she was burned alive before she ever found the resting places of the beloved husband and son. Some say she continues her search to this day.

Another account of the legend has a young couple living in a cabin that doubled as a stage coach stop in the mid-1800s. The Indians living in the area felt a deep resentment for the encroachment. It was built on sacred ground used by their ancestors a thousand years earlier for spiritual purposes. They planned an attack. They surrounded the cabin, tortured the young couple, and burned the structure to the ground. However, before her demise, the young woman was able to hide her two young children in the hollow of an old oak tree, praying they would not be found. The young children were found the next day and taken to safety. Sadly, the mother does not know. She wanders the valley, longing for her children, many times atop a beautiful white horse.

One unfortunate carload of teenagers got more than they bargained for on their "cruise." As they rounded a curve in the road, they suddenly became aware of a lady on a white horse She was engulfed in

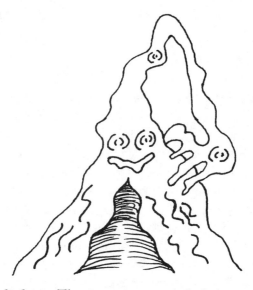

bright lights. The image so startled the young driver he lost control of the car and it rolled over. When the police arrived, the excited youths told the officer what they had seen. Usually a confession of this sort would warrant an arrest for driving under the influence. But it was clear to the officer the teens were visibly shaken, not intoxicated. As the officer inspected the wreckage, the headlights mysteriously started blinking on and off. A short, no doubt, he thought. But you will never convince the frightened teenagers it was not the Lady in White confirming her visit. They were not alone in their terrifying experience. There are about twenty accidents along Harmony Grove and Questhaven roads each year. Many are blamed on the Lady in White.

Another group of young people were cruising the area one moonless night when they met the eerie apparition. They bravely summoned up the courage to confront the spirit. She was bathed in a light so intense they could clearly see each others' faces even though the night was as black as velvet. It was so strangely silent they could hear the pounding of their heartbeats. The White Lady's robes gracefully billowed around her, and her eyes blazed a fiery red. She slowly raised her arm and summoned the group to leave. They hurriedly returned to the car and prepared to run the apparition down. They never had the chance, for the image faded before their eyes.

The Lady in White sometimes takes on different forms. She is often seen as a low cloud that silently floats up and down the creek. Some have seen her as a gently glowing white light fleeting among the trees.

While she is clearly the most celebrated ghost in the area, she is not the only uncommon occurrence in this most unusual valley. For years there have been sightings of an old English bellringer who roams the neighborhood. And there is a local legend that there is an entire Indian tribe that is buried in the valley. Each member is said to have been buried standing straight up. Locals have looked out of their windows on a dewy, misty morning to see young Indian children playing at the site of the giant grave. One woman repeatedly awoke to find her horse damp and breathless, as if it had been ridden hard all night. The horse's mane had been neatly braided. She never did discover who, or what was taking the animal out for these midnight outings.

The Elfin Forest, Harmony Grove area can be a place of extreme tranquility. It is a place devoid of crowds, crime, and other vices associated with city living. The people who live there have developed a real sense of community, and they know what it means to be good neighbors. It is not unusual for a small group to gather at the tiny Elfin Forest store on a warm summer night in a feeling of fellowship. The women share family recipes while the children play. The men

51

swap stories, of ancestors now departed, local history, and in general of what life was like before freeways, shopping malls, and large apartment complexes. And many times the talk will turn to the darker side of this beautiful valley. The side that harbors a beautiful spirit searching in vain for something she had lost during her young lifetime. The legend lives on.

Elfin Forest Vacation Park
7841 Harmony Grove Road
The White Lady can be seen throughout the area and along the creek.
See map, page 43.

Villa Montezuma

The Villa Montezuma
Jesse Shepard, Phantom of the Villa

It was destined to be the last time Jesse Shepard would ever play the piano. He was accustomed to playing for crowds of high society, Europeans, even royalty. As a young man he won rave reviews for his musical improvisations, in America as well as abroad. A life of wealth was routine for this most remarkable man. But now, he was alone in the slums of Los Angeles. He had found it necessary to sell his watch only a few days earlier. Playing one of his own compositions, his sensitive hands glided effortlessly over the keyboard. He was almost at the end of a magnificent crescendo when his hands suddenly froze on an unresolved seventh chord. He stiffened for an instant, then slumped over the piano. Jesse Shepard was dead.

*   *   *

Most people do a double take as they ascend the hill approaching the Villa Montezuma on K Street in the historic area of Golden Hill. What greets them is one of the most ornate buildings on the west coast. It is completely foreign to the other modest buildings in the area. Adorned with two mismatched towers, covered with stained glass windows, and topped with menacing grinning gargoyles, it is a supreme example of eclectic Victorian architecture.

It was built in 1887, another product of San Diego's "boom" years. Local citizens wanted a place of culture and art in the midst of the more rowdy nature of the young city. So some enterprising civic leaders got together to build a "Palace to the Arts."

They already knew who was going to live there before they even started. The building was erected to honor famed musician and writer, Jesse Shepard. Shepard had a following in San Diego not only because of his legendary musical abilities, but also because he was a known spiritualist.

Jesse Shepard was born in London. His family moved to America when he was only one year old, but the old world left its imprint on his young mind. He returned to Europe to give concerts and to study literature in France. His improvisational music won raves and he gave recitals before royalty in Europe and Alexander II of Russia.

When he returned to America he was lured to San Diego not only to give the city culture, but also to be an official greeter to visiting dignitaries. City boosters felt a celebrity in the neighborhood would also raise the price of land, and it did.

Jesse was no stranger to wealth and the good life. The prospect of living in the magnificent home greatly appealed to him. It was built to his specifications, right down to the stained glass windows of his favorite composers, Mozart and Beethoven. From the elegant drawing room to the grand music room, the house had Jesse's stamp on it. It was filled with beautiful books on art and literature. Upstairs, he had a museum filled with mementos and trophies of his triumphs in Europe. From the top of the observatory he could gaze out over the bay and watch the building of another of San Diego's jewels, the Hotel del Coronado.

Jesse was a beautiful man who particularly appealed to the fair maidens in town. He was a gentle soul with dreamy eyes and love of poetry. He completely charmed the citizens of San Diego with his worldly sophistication. Local ladies finally had occasion to buy fancy ball gowns. He threw extravagant musical galas and recitals that left the town talking for weeks. Because of his love of the occult, he also conducted seances, which thrilled the other spiritualists in town.

Jesse lived in this magical environment for only two years. When the boom years were over, even high society no longer had the money for such extravagance. The young rowdy town was really not to Jesse's liking anyway. After all, Jesse with his classic upbringing, was well above the likes of a place where Wyatt Earp had three saloons and gambling parlors not far away. Jesse elegantly waved a fond farewell to San Diego and headed back to Europe where he was still riding a wave of popularity.

In Europe Jesse wrote fine essays and gave concerts. However, as with all of us, his age caught up with him and his popularity began to fade. He returned from Europe this time to Los Angeles, a poor and broken man. He sold his watch given to him by King Edward VII, and died in the middle of his last recital in front of only the fewest guests.

The Villa Montezuma was never the same after Jesse left. It was sold and resold, no one having any success with the property. Then in March of 1986 a fire devastated the building, nearly burning it to the ground. The San Diego Historical Society, which operates the Villa, set up a restoration fund to raise money to save the building. They were very successful. Over a hundred artists, architects, designers, and specialists worked diligently to restore it to its original glory.

Jesse Shepard's house now stands proudly, not only as an historical monument, but as a museum. San Diego is much indebted to this most unusual man. He brought refinement and culture to a small town when it was much needed. He gave the town art, music, and excitement. He also gave it a haunted house...

*   *   *

From the start there have been legends revolving around this unusual building. Its appearance helps to promote these beliefs. It is the very image of a Victorian haunted house. Gargoyles grin down mysteriously at the approaching visitor. The large towers, while beautiful, sometimes seem strangely menacing against a bright blue sky. In its presence one is greeted with a feeling of mystery.

It is rumored that a man hung himself many years ago in the observatory tower. One version states that it was an overly sensitive butler of Jesse Shepard. Another tells of a young man so devastated over the death of his new wife he took the only way out. Whatever story you wish to believe, it is said that from the observatory window his body still can be seen hanging helplessly from a rope.

The neighbors surrounding the Villa will not hesitate to tell you that Halloween is a nightly event. They report seeing ghostly faces peering from the windows at all hours of the night.

One of the most unusual occurrences in the Villa involves the stained glass picture of the artist Peter Paul Rubens. As the years go by, his beard is slowly graying. Both tourists and staff members notice, but can give no logical explanation for this strange event.

Volunteers are baffled about a certain corner of the house. All over the dwelling, plants flourish, brightening the sometime dark corners. But in one area, nothing will grow. They have tried the heartiest of water-resistant plants, to no avail. What happened in that corner to make it so unwelcome to living things?

The Villa is the ultimate in mysterious mansions. All of the typical attributes of a haunted house apply here. Rumors of buried treasure, secret passageways, and concealed spaces behind all the fireplaces add up to a true place of mystery. Even the resident cat is a

step out of the ordinary. After the devastating fire all assumed that the pet had gone on to his reward up in cat heaven. But during the restoration, they found him, strolling around as if nothing had happened. He is a silver Abyssinian with blue eyes, a combination that should not even exist. He has an extra toe on every foot. This unusual pet has been a part of the Villa for sixteen years. It is not known which one of his nine lives he is on at this time. His name? Psyche.

People feel "things" in the rooms of this unusual house. What it is they do not know. Most are aware of some kind of presence that follows them from room to room. A group of school children found this out on a tour of the house. One young man strayed from his classmates while looking around upstairs. Something must have spooked the child, for he hurriedly ran to find his classmates. They were found huddled together in front of one of the many mirrors in the house. Nervously looking over their shoulders, they were frightened by some unseen force. This is one historic site the class is not looking forward to visiting again.

Rumor attributes these strange occurrences to the spirit of Jesse Shepard himself. The concerts he gave were not your average musical event. Jesse believed that souls of past, great musicians worked through his body when he played the piano in a trancelike state. He gave his guests quite a show.

He would greet his guests at his lavish parties with his usual charm and sophistication. After he had them thoroughly fascinated and under his spell, he led them into the music room. He dimmed the lights and took his place at the piano seat. What followed left the guests completely astounded. He would begin to play the most beautiful music they had ever heard, seemingly improvising as he went along. His body would gracefully sway along with the melody. Then as if by magic, people began to hear a choir of heavenly voices, distant at first, then getting louder, as if they were in the same room. Some people reported hearing drums, tambourines and trumpets play along with the music. Then the chorus would gradually fade away, leaving the guests to wonder where it had come from in the first place. The lights would appear, and there was Jesse, dramatically taking his bows to an excited audience.

Jesse was also famous for his seances. The many spiritualists in San Diego who admired Jesse always knew where to go when they wanted to make contact with a long-lost relative. Always the showman, Jesse claimed he could also communicate with Beethoven, Julius Caesar, and William Shakespeare. Only the best for Jesse.

After Jesse left for Europe, the house was home to many different owners. Because so many of them experienced difficulties after living in the house, it was thought to be jinxed.

One owner was the vice president of an important bank. He ended up in Europe, not on vacation, but as a fugitive running from justice. Even the president of the bank could not be free from the spell of the house. He committed suicide about the same time his associate went on his unscheduled trip. The next owners found they could no longer make sound business decisions. Without explanation, they ended up bankrupt, losing the house through foreclosure. Disaster after disaster awaited the next couple. The wife reported her husband became more reckless as time went by. A giant gray cloud began to engulf the couple and a considerable fortune was lost. The husband, no longer able to withstand the pressure, disappeared, never to be heard from again. One of the owners happened to be another spiritualist. He told of strange sounds at all hours of the night. Music coming from the pipes, tapping noises, and moaning and sobbing disrupted his sleep on a regular basis.

After these misfortunes became more public, all

the old rumors that the house is haunted resurfaced. Speculation was that Jesse was back in town. Or possibly the man that hung himself in the observatory tower was now enjoying the beautiful view of the city from this high point. Shadowy forms were seen roaming the house and the neighborhood children wouldn't go near it.

Today the spell of bad luck has been broken. It is again a happy, beautiful, cultured place, as it was during the two years when Jesse Shepard lived here. About 20,000 people a year visit this beautiful Victorian jewel, and many joyful occasions are celebrated here. It cannot be duplicated as a better, more romantic setting for a wedding, reception, or anniversary party. The San Diego Historical Society operates the museum in top form and it is restored to its original splendor. It is especially exquisite during the holiday season when it is decked in the colors of the season. An afternoon tea is usually held, and the house lives up to its reputation as a palace to the arts.

Still, the rumors persist. One cannot ignore the reports of curious happenings within the walls of this historic home. Go see it for yourself. Admire the exquisite furnishings, decorations, and artifacts. And if the spirit moves you, sit down at the lovely piano in the music room. You may want to finally resolve that dominant seventh chord Jesse left hanging in time when he left this world.

The Villa Montezuma
1925 K Street
12:00 to 4:30 Saturday & Sunday.
Times and days subject to change.
See map, page 31.

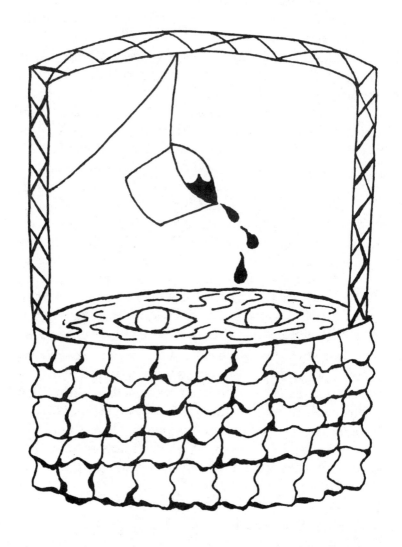

Casa de Estudillo

Casa de Estudillo

A temporary look at a permanent reflection

It was the perfect afternoon for a wedding. The sun filtered through the leaves and left a dappled effect on the elaborately decorated patio. A gentle breeze carried the sweet scent of hibiscus and honeysuckle through the warm air. Everywhere you could hear the sounds of birds chirping happily. The bride walked slowly to the wishing well where she would exchange vows with her betrothed. She was lovely in a traditional Mexican wedding dress. For luck, she tossed a penny into the famous wishing well. She leaned over to watch the ripples in the water when she began to feel faint. The face she saw in the water was not her own! Her brown hair was replaced by thick black braids and the eyes staring back at her were of the clearest blue she had ever seen. Her world started spinning and she collapsed to the ground in a dead faint.

*   *   *

The Casa De Estudillo was the first lavish family home built in the little Pueblo of San Diego in the year 1827. It was planned by one of early California's most predominant families. Jose Maria Estudillo, a general, was the Commandant of the Presidio in Monterey as well as the Presidio in San Diego. Born of noble Spanish ancestry, the distinguished leader was completing a military career of more than thirty years when he acquired some land through a grant. It was located in the plaza of Old Town. It was owned "in common" with his son-in-law Juan Bandini, a member of another of San Diego's first families.

Jose Maria's son, Jose Antonio Estudillo, built the house to honor his wife Maria Victoria. He was also a leader in early San Diego history. Through the years he served as treasurer, tax collector, alcade, or mayor, and county assessor.

The house became widely known as the Casa De Estudillo. The governor of Alta California lived in San Diego at the time. This gave Jose Antonio the political clout to build such an impressive home. It was one of the finest homes of the period. It recalled the romantic, colorful era of the Spanish Dons.

The adobe walls were five feet thick to protect the inhabitants from the cold as well as heat. The roof was covered with Spanish tile. Rawhide held the mighty beams in place. It had twelve rooms, including a chapel. The house enclosed a beautiful spacious patio where generations of Estudillo children laughed and played.

For fifty years the house was a social and cultural center for the young town. Family and friends would gather in the cupola to observe the many colorful events that were staged on the plaza.

During the Mexican War, the Estudillo family remained neutral. Their home was used as a refuge for frightened women and children. The chapel became a place of meditation for those fearful for the lives of their loved ones.

After the war, the home again became a recreational center. However, times were changing in the growing town of San Diego. Alonzo Horton built a waterfront hamlet that became known as "New Town." Old Town found itself in economic trouble when most of its inhabitants moved to the new area.

The town and buildings slowly began to decay. The last of the Estudillo family was gone by 1887.

Circumstances looked pretty grim for the historic home until an event happened that would change its future forever. A book was written by Helen Hunt Jackson called *Ramona* .

Jackson had come to SanDiego to do research for an historic novel. She was also here as an activist on behalf of Indian rights. She teamed up with Father Anthony Ubach who was a priest living at the Estudillo house. He too was in favor of the fair treatment of Indians, and tended to be rather militant about it. They enjoyed many long talks about their common interest at the Estudillo home.

Some say that the stories told to her by Father Ubach inspired her to write the tragic story of Ramona. The novel involves an illegitimate, beautiful half-Indian girl and her Indian lover, Alessandro. Alessandro was helplessly drawn to the lovely Ramona, with her ink black hair and sky blue eyes. While it is a tragic love story, it also tells of the brutal intrusion of the white settlers into the Indian community and how they stripped them of their proud culture. This gave the author a chance to vent her own strong feelings about the mistreatment of Indians. Her book had a political impact as well as a literary one. Because it was read by so many people it influenced the way people began to feel about the Indian culture. It paved the way for Congress to pass the Dawes Act, a bill that eventually gave the Indians the right to citizenship.

Father Ubach evidently left his impression on the author. He was responsible for starting the Church of the Immaculate Conception in Old Town, which still stands today. The Padre was a militant sort, outspoken about his views, and more than a little fond of good Spanish red wine. In the novel it is a Father Gaspara that marries Ramona and Alessandro, but it is clear that she modeled the soldier-like Gaspara after the aggressive Father Ubach.

For localities she used real places such as Santa Barbara, Temecula, and San Diego. So real in fact were her characters and locales, her faithful readers assumed the entire book was based on fact. Brochures were put out in the various places where events happened in the book to help promote tourist trade. To her fans, this only served to reinforce the idea that Ramona and Alessandro were true lovers.

The description of the home in which Father Gaspara married the star-crossed lovers fit the old Estudillo home. It was a one-story building on the plaza, and the only Catholic chapel in town. This just had to be the marriage place of Ramona. This conception was further helped along by the caretaker in charge of the decaying building. He promoted the Ramona story and sold tiles, bricks, door keys, and anything he could get his hands on to tourists anxious to have a souvenir of the marriage place of their heroine. When he completed his looting, the once beautiful building stood in ruin.

A predominant businessman, John Spreckels, bought the building after reading Ramona. He had the foresight to see what a profitable business venture this could be for the declining economy of Old Town. After a complete restoration, the building reopened under the name of Ramona's Marriage Place. A trolley car stop was provided for easy access and soon it became a popular tourist attraction, complete with a souvenir store and restaurant. But it was romance, instead of the commercial aspect, that made it such a success. Thousands of couples wanted to be married in the same place that united their beloved Ramona and Alessandro.

The building was leased to Thomas Getz, a former theatre manager with a flair for the dramatic. He was completely taken with the Ramona story and elaborated on the romantic aspect. He told sensitive stories about the wishing well and the marriage chapel that enthralled his audiences and helped to make the attraction even more famous. It became so well known that several silent movies were filmed in the celebrated adobe.

Because of the success of Ramona's Marriage Place, Old Town experienced a rebirth of other restorations. New businesses opened to help accommodate the growing tourist trade. Effort was made to capture the romance of old Mexico in building restaurants, curio shops, and plaza activities. Old Town began to attract visitors on its own merit.

The building was restored a second time in 1967 and was purchased by the state as part of the Old Town Historic Park. The state thought that the house had become too commercialized and its true history had been lost. Much care was taken this time to make sure the restoration was true to the Estudillo family rather than the story of Ramona.

During the city's 200th year celebration, house was re-christened "The Casa De Estudillo." A gala dedication ceremony was planned to open the house to the public. On hand were three direct descendants of the original Estudillo family who watched as their family home was honored.

The Ramona's Marriage Place sign has long been torn down. Some say it was a mistake to promote the house as a commercial endeavor because it distorted history. But it is doubtful that the house would now be such a popular museum had it not been widely regarded as the marriage place of Ramona first. The story has become part of Old Town's folklore and people hope the spirit of Ramona never leaves. Apparently she hasn't, for many tourists and the staff at the Casa De Estudillo claim the place is haunted...

*   *   *

The young bride recovered and was able to go on with the wedding. The rings and vows were exchanged without further interruptions. The couple enjoyed their beautiful reception and after a glass or two of champagne, the young woman began to feel rather foolish. A face in the well, of all things! Her fainting spell was just a matter of pre-wedding jitters. However, before the young couple left for their honeymoon, she ventured over to the wishing well and peered in. Although this time the water was still and black, she knew that what she saw had not been an illusion.

The Casa De Estudillo does not have the image of a typical haunted house. With its white walls, tiled roof, and authentic Spanish furnishings, it recreates the days of early California. Its location on the plaza of Old Town gives it a festive atmosphere, especially in the summer when the plaza is filled with vacationers.

But many say the place is not as innocent as it looks. Unexplained noises occur all over the house, footsteps, objects dropping, and doors creaking are just a few of the sounds that greet some of the people that work there. The piano in the grand Sala, or living room, will sometimes have an invisible musician at its bench playing traditional Mexican music, much

68

like in the days when the house was the social center of Old Town. One worker tells of the time when a music box opened of its own accord and played her a lovely tune.

Another occurrence is that of a shadowy figure that flitters across the walls. More than one visitor has been startled by a dark shape that passes before their eyes as they tour the house. Upon turning to see if someone is there, they find that they are alone. This happens most often in the Indian work room, leading some people to think Alessandro may still be around, searching for his beautiful Ramona.

Many people have been startled to look in one of the bedroom mirrors only to see a face other than their own. Most often it is that of a young Mexican man, presumably one of the Estudillo family. The priest's bedroom boasts a large wooden cabinet with mirrored doors. Many times an image is seen that closely resembles that of Father Anthony Ubach.

The famous wishing well has long been a place of peace and tranquillity. As you take the walk along the brick paved path through the beautiful garden that leads to the wishing well, you just might feel the presence of all the brides that have walked the path before. As you stand by the well under its wooden canopy covered with vines, you may be overcome with a feeling of happiness and well-being. The well itself has been planted with ferns to discourage any more fainting spells from young brides surprised to see the haunting eyes of Ramona gazing back at them.

The house is a mix of unusual experiences. One young man was surprised to walk into someone, or so he thought. He felt a force that would not allow him to pass, but to his amazement no one was there. Glimmers of red light have been noted in the master bedroom with no apparent cause. The house possesses cold spots. One man suffered such an icy sensation that he shivered, even though it was a warm spring day. The Mexican bake oven located outside of the kitchen sometimes produces the enticing smell of bread baking. The only problem is that it is no longer in use.

Once a visitor brought his expensive camera equipment so he could capture the atmosphere of early California on film. He didn't get quite the atmosphere he was after. His state of the art lens dropped out of his camera bag and crashed to the floor. Upon examining the bag he found that the lens had been stored in a deep compartment and could not have fallen out by itself. But it did. He replaced it, and even shook the bag upside down to see if it would slip out. It held tight. Clearly some ghostly creature was a little camera shy.

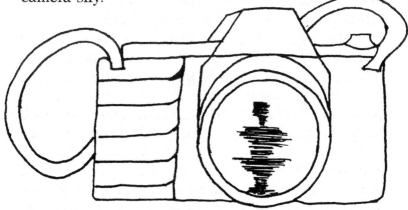

Perhaps the most unsettling event in the house is the mysterious voice. Visitors have distinctly heard a male voice order them to "GET OUT!" It is a deep husky command that startles those who experience it. Some feel it may be the voice of Father Ubach, still angry over the bigotry of some uncaring people.

The Casa De Estudillo possesses a sense of history with its beautiful period furnishings and artifacts. The Colonial Dames of San Diego are greatly responsible for the care and upkeep of this historic home, as well as keeping the legacy of early California alive.

There is no denying the sense of romance as one takes the worn path to the romantic wishing well. A feeling of sweet whimsy captures many as the recall the devotion of the stunning Ramona and her beloved Alessandro.

But the Casa also possesses a sense of mystery with its unexplained sounds and occurrences. Just who are the spirits that dwell within its celebrated adobe walls? Perhaps the answer is lost in the romance of the past. When you visit the Casa De Estudillo, enjoy all the beauty and history it has to offer, but be prepared to make a quick exit when a menacing voice tells you to "GET OUT!"

Casa De Estudillo
In the middle of the plaza, Old Town
Daily, 10:00 a.m. to 4:00 p.m.
Times and days subject to change.
See map, page 17.

Heritage Park

Heritage Park
Toyland: Returns Welcome

The beautiful young homemaker wanted to find the perfect Christmas present for her eight-year-old daughter. She decided to try a little doll shop she had heard about located in a Victorian village. She was exhausted from a full day of shopping. Her feet hurt and her head was beginning to ache. Scrooge had nothing on her, she thought with a grimace. But as she climbed the stairs to the shop, a feeling of peace and well-being began to overcome her. A sense of wonder enveloped her as she slowly wandered through the rooms filled with doll houses, toys, and everything a little girl could ever want. She was drawn to the room filled with the most life-like dolls she had ever seen. Hundreds of tiny eyes peered at her from every corner of the beautiful room. In a trance-like state she walked over to a doll nearly hidden in a corner. The doll was a little girl dressed in a forest green Victorian dress. She had long red hair, eyes like emeralds, and a dusting of freckles across her ivory skin. Unconsciously, the young woman reached up and brushed a lock of her own red hair away from her face. She knew she had found the perfect gift for her daughter. What she didn't know was that she had found a gift for herself as well. Upon leaving the shop, she was completely at peace with the world, humming Christmas carols, eager to get home to her family, a stark contrast to the woman who had entered only a few moments before.

*   *   *

We live in an age where people think anything old is worthless. In the name of progress seasoned buildings are destroyed to make way for shopping malls, parking lots, and freeways. Thankfully, this is not the norm in a beautiful little corner of San Diego known as Heritage Park.

In the 1960s a Victorian house known as the Sherman-Gilbert was destined to be destroyed to make way for a parking lot. A concerned group of citizens formed an organization to save the building. They were known as the Save Our Heritage Organizaion, or SOHO. The county acquired almost eight acres of the Old Town State Park in 1970 and Heritage Park was born.

The Sherman-Gilbert house sat in ruin for three years until the Board of Supervisors could raise funds to restore it. It now stands as a tribute to San Diego's romantic Victorian age. It boasts the only "widows walk" left in the area. A widows walk is a walkway on which wives could go up and watch for their seagoing husbands to return from the sea. Sadly, sometimes they did not appear, hence the name.

After the first restoration was complete, others followed. All types of Victorian architecture are represented. The Bushyhead House is known as Italianate and the Christian House typical Queen Anne. The McConaughy is known as a stick style and the Burton House is classic revival. There is even a modest cottage that houses an office where volunteers happily give out information about the park. One truly unique building in the park is the Temple Beth Israel, with its stained glass windows and beautiful columns. It is the oldest standing synagogue in Southern California.

An unusual feature of the park is the way the

buildings are used. Instead of having the restored houses serve as museums, they are working businesses. Leases have been granted to small shops and facilities that were typical of the Victorian age. The Sherman-Gilbert House is the home of a quaint doll shop. A travel agency is located in the Burton House. A charming old-fashioned office is used for attorneys' quarters in the McConaughy House. The Christian House is home to a delightful bed and breakfast inn that also includes a lovely restaurant that is especially popular for a Sunday brunch.

Heritage Park beautifully recreates a Victorian community in both architecture and atmosphere. It is a captivating place for a walk on a sunny afternoon. Stop in at the Christian House for a spot of tea. Take time to sit on the stone benches and admire the buildings that take you back to another era that should never be forgotten. One thing for sure. The spirits of San Diego have not forgotten Heritage Park. Two of its houses are rumored to be haunted...

*   *   *

Some people find shopping at Ye Old Doll Shoppe in the Sherman-Gilbert House a mystical experience. Whatever presence occupies this charming store, it is a non-threatening one. All the staff members agree that there is something about the store that gives people

a feeling of peace and happiness. One lady who used to work for the store admitted she was usually afraid to be alone, especially at night. But for some reason, this was not true when she was in the store, even after hours. She could not explain it, but she stated a feeling of extreme happiness came over her when it came time to lock up for the day. Other people and staff members have had the same uncanny experience.

Another curious event sometimes occurs in the room where all the dolls are displayed. Like the woman who was looking for a Christmas present for her daughter, some people are mysteriously drawn to one doll in particular. There are hundreds of dolls in this room, all shapes, sizes, and ages, and all remarkably life-like. They each display a unique personality, some thoughtful, some playful, and some impish. With so many staring eyes, it is not hard to see why some people are a little spooked. But a lucky few will set their eyes on a doll and lose sight of all others.

They are not aware of the fact that the doll they are drawn to is the essence of themselves when they were a young child. The red-haired lady needed to have that particular doll, not just because they had the same hair, but because the doll recaptured the joyful spirit that she used to be. Perhaps this strange occurrence accounts for the peaceful aura of this most unusual shop. For a select circle, they are not just buying a doll, they are finding their lost childhood.

There is another interesting house in Heritage Park that stands in stark contrast to the idyllic feeling of the Sherman-Gilbert. It is the McConaughy House. It is home to a group of lawyers who simply love to finish up their business before nightfall.

All admit there are sounds that cannot be

explained in any logical manner. This is a very hard fact for the legal mind to comprehend. One attorney over several weeks kept hearing footsteps upstairs. Time after time he would call out to see who was on the upper floor. After no one responded, he would go up to check for himself. No one was ever there.

Other noises disturb the tenants as well. There are sounds of something brushing up against the walls outside. They wouldn't give it another thought, except there are no trees standing near the building that could produce the sound.

None of the lawyers like to work there late. When they do some strange sound usually sends them home early. They all admit they have a most unique place to perform their legal services.

San Diego has done a wonderful job in preserving her Victorian past. Each building in Heritage Park is distinctive, with its own character. Two of them are different in a most unusual way. It is best to visit the Burton House first. Afterward, if your nerves are rattled by unexplained noises, you can stop by Ye Old Doll Shoppe. If you're one of the lucky ones, you can regain that sense of wonderment that is hidden within us all.

Heritage Park is located on Juan Street in Old Town. See map, page 17.

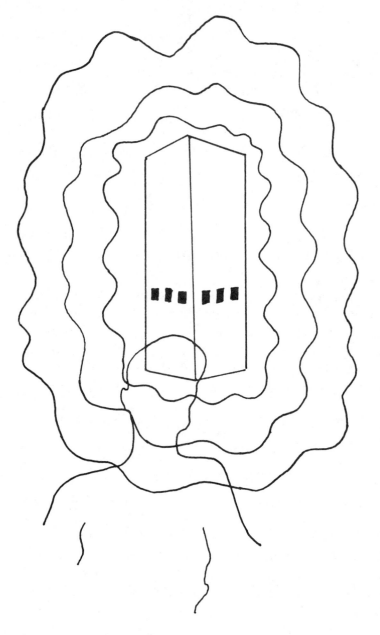

Wells Fargo Bank

The Wells Fargo Bank Building
Old Wells Fargo Bankers never die, they just enter different stages

The custodian never did like performing his duties on the eighth floor of the massive bank building in downtown San Diego. The eighth floor always made him feel a little uneasy, but tonight the feeling was intense. The hour didn't help. He was running more than an hour late and the long hallways seemed darker than usual. The soft fluorescent lights above provided little light and seemed to have a menacing glow. The best thing he could do was to hurry through his chores and get off that floor as soon as possible. He wished he could erase from his mind the theme song from the "Twilight Zone." A sigh of relief welled up inside when he was at the end of his task. As he turned to leave, he froze in his tracks. There was a man standing at the other end of the hallway staring at him intently. He knew that all the tenants had left the building hours ago. The man stood there a moment longer, then turned and disappeared into one of the offices. Because of the late hour, the custodian considered calling security. Instead, he summoned up all his courage and went to the door and knocked. Surely the intruder could be persuaded to leave the premises peacefully. When there was no response, he tried the door. It was locked, so he used his passkey to enter the office. Nervously he switched on the lights and looked everywhere. Nothing was out of order and there were no broken windows. He stood there in disbelief. On the eighth floor there was only one way out. But still, the room was empty.

* * *

Modern downtown San Diego has its beginnings in the early 1850s. There was a need to move the growing city from its origin in "Old Town" to the waterfront. The first person to attempt this was William Heath Davis in 1851. He bought 163 acres and tried to establish a "New Town" closer to the bay. He launched an elaborate promotion campaign that tried to convince the people this was the area of the future. He failed miserably. Died in the wool Old Towners dubbed the fiasco "Davis's Folly."

A number of years later a much more successful attempt was launched. A San Francisco businessman, Alonzo Horton, heard of San Diego's wonderful bay area. It became his dream to build a prosperous waterfront city there. He bought 960 acres for what would make current real estate people roll their eyes in disbelief. But in those days the waterfront property was practically worthless. This land was destined to become one of the most successful cities in the state of California.

For a time it was the Fifth Avenue area that was the hub of the downtown scene. Some of the city's most glamourous office buildings were built along this street. Later, Broadway became the center of action while Fifth Avenue sat in decay. Great care has been taken to restore these areas so tourists and locals alike can sit at outdoor cafes and enjoy the facades of these wonderful buildings. One of the best spots to absorb the ambience of early San Diego is the historic Gaslamp District.

Today the city is a mecca for tourists at all times of the year. For the culturally inclined, there is the San Diego Symphony and Opera. Summer nights are filled with music as the Starlight Bowl program gears into full swing. The historic Old Globe Theatre puts on its fine productions in the fall. Balboa Park is home to the city's finest museums. These include the San Diego Museum of Art, the distinguished Timken Gallery, the Reuben H. Fleet Space Theatre, and the Natural History Museum. Many of the buildings were built for the Panama-California Exposition in 1915. The San Diego Zoo is world renowned, not only for its magnificent display of animals, but also for its efforts to protect endangered species.

The downtown skyline has changed dramatically over the last few years. Today modern architecture coexists with historic restorations in perfect harmony. The Convention Center with its sensational ship-like appearance and curved glass windows makes a powerful statement on the waterfront. New office buildings and hotels are both unusual and artistic. These new buildings, plus all the other attractions the city has to offer, put San Diego in a class with the finest cities in the United States. Alonzo Horton's dream has been beautifully realized.

One building that dots the San Diego skyline deserves special attention. The Wells Fargo Bank, formerly the Great American Bank building is perhaps the most unusual modern building in the city. Outwardly there is nothing strange about it. But inside, on the eighth floor, there is a presence that refuses to leave...

*   *   *

A haunted bank building? The idea seems outrageous in a city filled with buildings that better fit the image of a haunted house. But try to tell that to a number of people who work there and they will heartily disagree.

After the custodian had the encounter with the apparition on the eighth floor, he vowed to remain silent for fear people would think he had taken leave of his senses. He later decided to tell a fellow worker about his unusual experience. He fully expected some intense ribbing, but instead he got a serious response. The same thing had happened to his friend a week earlier! The stories were the same, down to the last detail.

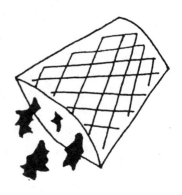

After a while, more people began to come forward with tales of strange happenings. It was not only the custodians that had stories to tell.

One of the tenants was working very late in his office one night when he heard the outside door open. Thinking it was his partner, he called out to see why anyone else would want to work at this late hour. He didn't get a response. He later noticed his partner's phone line was on. Feeling something was amiss, he decided to investigate. He went to the other office and found light coming from under the door and heard a conversation going on. However, when he entered the office, no one was present and the phone was not in use. Thinking he was just overworked, he went back to his office for a strong cup of coffee. He found the phone line was on again. Back down the hall, he found the lights were on again. He knew for sure he had turned them off. He tried the door, but found it locked from the inside. About this time, he decided it was time to call it a night. It was the last time he would ever stay alone in the office.

While some of the people who work there are alarmed about the ghost that haunts the building, most of them are not really too concerned about the intruder. In fact, some of them find having a ghost around can be a big help. Sometimes the janitors will arrive at an office to clean up and find the task has already been done for them. Waste baskets have been emptied, ashtrays cleaned, and desktops are left shining. Some report the sound of a ghostly vacuum cleaner running on the floor below them.

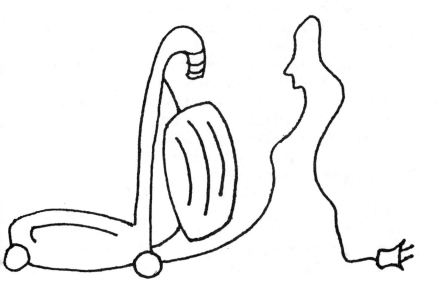

While most of the activity is located on the eighth floor, other areas also experience some spooky happenings. Once, an entire office staff on the sixteenth floor was amazed when they returned to work after a long weekend. All of the office furniture had been rearranged. Nothing was where it had been. Even the pictures had been moved to different locations. The funny thing about it is they like this new arrangement much better as they have more room and the visual effect is much more pleasing. This is one ghost with a flair for decorating.

One lucky photgrapher ran into the ghost on the twelfth floor. He was determined to get a picture of whatever was responsible for all the excitement in the building. He staged an all-night stakeout. He was not disappointed. In the middle of the night, he saw a transparent image approach him slowly. As it got closer and closer, the man started taking a series of pictures. He was so scared that his hands were shaking and he hardly knew what he was doing. Then, suddenly, the image faded away right in front of him. When the film was developed there was a picture of part of a man walking down the hall. It was taken to an expert in parapsychology at a local university to be verified. It is considered to be one of the best pictures of an apparition ever taken.

It is not clear who the ghost is that haunts the downtown building. Most people feel it is a former employee who may have come on desperate times after losing his job at the bank. In any case, most people regard him with a sense of humor. They feel that he is an asset in an already pleasant working atmosphere, and he sets their building apart from all the other bank buildings in town.

There is much to do when visiting the downtown area of San Diego. Beautiful Balboa Park for joggers, Horton Plaza for the shoppers, and Seaport Village for atmosphere and fine waterfront dining. The Gaslamp District for the history buffs and the Embarcadero provide pleasant afternoon walks all through the year. And if the mood strikes you, drop in at the Wells Fargo Bank to cash a check, open an account, or perhaps run into a spectral banker. The building may be strangely out of character for a haunting, but in reality it is a shell for an old-fashioned ghost story.

Wells Fargo Bank
600 B Street
Downtown San Diego
See map, page 31.

Presidio Park

Presidio Park
Once a deer, always a dear

Her name was Lucy and she was totally white in color. The little white deer spent her days playfully romping through the canyons and hills of the serene park. Her park. The residents of the area would leave fruit and other goodies for her to dine on in their yards. At night she would sometimes startle young lovers who would use the park for a romantic hideaway. Her white form was striking against the greenblackness of the park's beautiful landscaping. No one had ever tried to hurt her so she had no fear of the humans that loved to share her park. So it was natural for her to be curious when she saw a man approach her carrying a gun.

Lucy had been getting braver about approaching the more populated areas of the park. People began to fear for the young doe's safety. If she could be tranquilized and moved to a more remote area, it would be in the animal's best interests. The animal control officer took care not to get too close and frighten her. He aimed and shot the tranquilizer gun. She looked startled, then fell softly to the ground. She was then gently transported to the Humane Society for observation. For a while Lucy held her own, but she later went into shock. The people in charge of her care felt for a heart beat, but there was none. Tears welled up in their eyes when they realized the dose had been too large for the beautiful doe. She looked so peaceful as she lay motionless, for she was no longer at the Humane Society, she was back in the park she called home.

*   *   *

A beautiful sight awaits the people that round the corner of Interstate 8 leading into Mission Valley. There, up on a hill surrounded by a lush park, sits the San Diego Presidio. It was at this spot, July 1, 1769, Father Junipero Serra recited mass for the survivors of the rigorous trip from Baja to Alta California. The purpose of the trip was the colonization of Alta California by Spain.

On July 16 a religious ceremony was conducted that formalized the first mission, San Diego De Alcala. It marked the birth of California.

Twenty more missions were to follow along the Camino Real up through California during the Spanish and Mexican periods. They were placed a day's journey apart by horse or donkey. Their purpose was to educate and assimilate the local Indians into a more civilized way of life and to introduce them to the Christian religion. They were also taught farming and other trades. Although there are reports of flogging of Indians by the padres, for the most part they were considered wards and were taken care of and treated well. At times, however, there was much rebellion on the part of the Indians who resented another culture being forced upon them. The purpose of the Presidio was to protect the missions from these hostile outbursts.

The tiny colony formed on Presidio Hill had its share of problems and the people suffered greatly during their first months here. A major Indian uprising took place and a stockade had to be built to protect both the colony and the mission. A more serious problem awaited the colonists in January 1770. No supplies had been sent from Spain and the settlement was near starvation. Each day a vigil took place, the people hoping and praying to see a ship's mast approach in the distance. By March they were about to give up hope and admit that the California venture was doomed to failure. Then on March 19 a miracle happened. Cheers welled up among the people as a supply ship eased its way into the bay. It was not only their salvation, but California's as well.

In a few months the stockade of the Presidio was completed, two cannons were installed, and some wooden houses were constructed. Soon there was a cemetery, a chapel, guard, and storehouses. The Commandant's home was in the center.

In 1774 Father Serra felt that the raucous behavior of some of the soldiers was too unsettling for his Indian charges. Also there was not a good water supply where the mission was located. He moved the mission to its present location six miles northeast, by the San Diego River.

By the end of the Spanish period, the settlement had grown to about 450 Spaniards and 6,800 Indian neophytes. The wooden Presidio was replaced with adobe buildings. By this time other missions were developed in the present Los Angeles and Monterey areas. The state of California was well on its way. However, under Mexican rule, the Presidio and military establishment began to decline rapidly. By 1839 the Presidio was in ruins.

It was George Marston, a local entrepreneur, who saved the Presidio, and is ultimately responsible for its beautiful appearance today. Always interested in park development, he acquired land at the site and donated it to the city. He also hired an architect to build a museum. His vision was realized in July 1929 at a ceremony on the 160th anniversary of Father Serra's dedication of the mission on the very same site.

Today the park is a hub of activity, a perfect place for family picnics. On any given Sunday, groups of children can be seen playing with their frisbees on the flat areas of the grassy knolls. It is also a popular place for spring and summer weddings. The Serra museum sits atop the hill as a grand monument to California's beginning. It is filled with fifteenth, sixteenth, and seventeenth century Spanish pieces. A giant cross sits proudly in the center of the park. It bears this inscription: "Here The First citizen, Fray Junipero Serra, Planted Civilization in California, Here He Raised the Cross, Here Began the First Mission, Here He Found the First Town—San Diego, July 16, 1769."

There is another monument in the park that does not go unnoticed by the local people. It is a tribute to Lucy, the little white deer whose spirit still roams the hillsides of the park she loves...

*   *   *

Lucy was born n the San Diego Zoo in 1965. A native of Southern Europe, she was striking, perfect in every way, and totally white in color. At the time the zoo had an over-population of its deer community, so Lucy was sold, with a buck, to a private individual who lived in Mission Hills. The young animals soon escaped from their confines for a life of freedom in and around Presidio Park.

The buck was never seen again, but Lucy became a local celebrity for ten years as she made the park her home. People thought of her as a pet, and everyone in the area took part in putting food out for her. No one even got mad when she feasted on her favorite treat, freshly planted zinnias, which locals referred to as "Lucy Salad."

Growing concern for her safety was at a height on a fateful night in December 1975. Lucy was trying to cross busy Taylor Street when the animal control officers started receiving calls urging them to rescue the celebrated deer and move her to safety.

After Lucy's tragic untimely death, the public was outraged. An investigation was put in effect on the officer who fired the deadly shot. But as time went by, people accepted the fact that their friend was gone through a devastating accident.

A year later a monument was dedicated to the beloved pet of Presidio Park. Money was raised for a memorial in her honor that would give tribute to wildlife. It is a shallow drinking pool placed atop Inspiration Point, a favorite spot of Lucy's. It is imbedded with the tracks of local small animals. It also has casts of Lucy's own hoofprints. At the dedication ceremony, tears were shed and stories were shared. Tributes were given by the county supervisor and a local English professor read a poem that celebrated the joys of wildlife.

Lucy has never been forgotten, and many people feel her spirit has never left the only home she ever knew. Some feel her presence at a family picnic, when they hear a rustling in the brush behind them. They turn, expecting to see the friendly pale form peeking out from the leaves, hoping for a piece of juicy fruit to enjoy on a warm summer evening. They smile when they remember her nightly visits to look for food. Some are sure they still hear her lurking about in the early evening hours.

When spring approaches, the Mission Hills area is ablaze with newly planted flowers. Some still insist on planting zinnias in their gardens. They are not the least bit surprised when they awake to find the new flowers have been dug up. Lucy's salad days are here again.

For years early morning joggers were used to seeing Lucy as they made their daily rounds. They would round a corner, hear the rustling of the bushes, and see a white tail disappear down a hill. This is still a common occurrence for runners today.

Lucy was never seen in the bright daylight and she still isn't. The best times to experience her are at twilight and the early morning hours. She would love to roam around as the mist and low clouds would settle on the rolling hills. Sometimes she can be seen as a wispy cloud scampering down one of her hills. She has startled more than one motorist as they were headed to work along the highway.

The legend of Lucy is well known in the Presidio Hills area. For those who knew her and loved her, she was more than a community pet. She was a symbol—a symbol of freedom and innocence and purity right in the center of a metropolitan area. She will forever be a part of this very beautiful park.

When you visit Presidio Park, stop in at the Serra Museum to get a taste of early California history. Take a leisurely walk around the park to view the various monuments. And don't leave without stopping at Inspiration Point to pay your respects to Lucy, the white deer that has captured the imagination of San

Diegans for years. With luck, you may get to see her for yourself.

The Serra Museum is located at Presidio Drive in the Old Town area. The park surrounds the museum. See map, page 17.

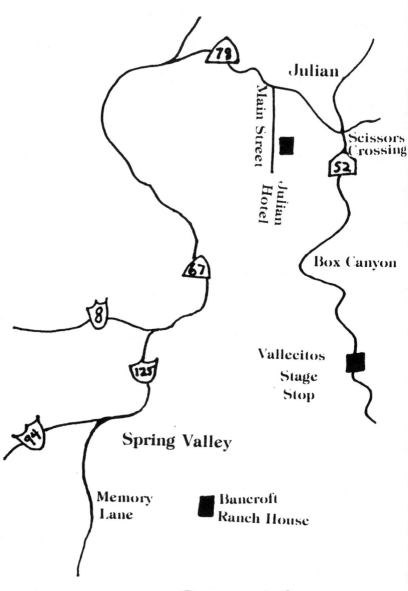

East County

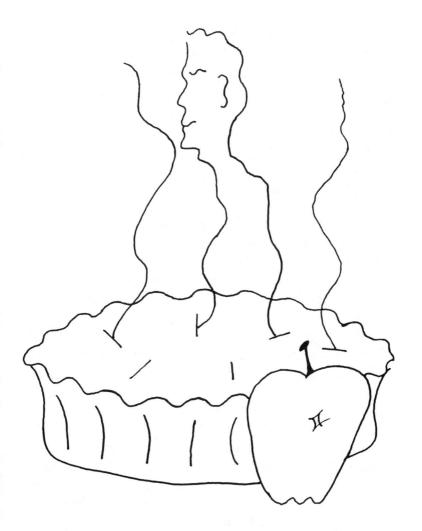

Julian Hotel

The Julian Hotel
They gave Albert the business, but he stayed for the pie.

Albert Robinson had suffered the indignities of bigotry his entire life. So when he moved his family to the tiny town of Julian, he didn't expect anything different. The little mining community was not known for its liberal attitudes toward AfricanAmericans. But Albert, a freed slave, was able to make a decent living for himself. With the help of his wife, he worked hard and established the Robinson Hotel. The hotel was an instant success and was popular with people traveling through the area on their way to San Diego. There was a stage coach stop across the street, and many of the drivers became regulars, eager to come in for a slice of Mrs. Robinson's warm apple pie. With a thriving business, Albert achieved some happiness and grew to love the little town of Julian. Albert did everything he could to gain some respect for himself from the townspeople. He thought he had, until the day he died. The town had a cemetery, but it was reserved only for whites. His widow was told her beloved husband had to be buried "with his own kind" at a cemetery out of town, far from the home he loved. Albert Robinson had been dealt his last, final humiliation.

*　　　　*　　　　*

Legend tells us a sentimental tale of the founding of the town of Julian. Four young men had been traveling for days when they arrived at an area in the hills above San Diego. It was late in the 1860s and the boys had been through the horrors of the Civil War. The beauty of the area so enchanted two of the tired young men they decided to travel no farther. With the help of their friends they established a homestead on a beautiful hillside among the majestic pines, oaks, and sycamores. They knew that the atmosphere of clean mountain air, furry animals running about, and solitude would help them put their war memories behind them. The other two young men decided the lure of the "city" was more to their liking, so they continued on to the pueblo of San Diego. Their parting was sweet, they had been through so much together they felt like brothers. The ones who stayed named their newly formed area "Julian" after one of their friends.

If this lovely story is true, the boys' solitude was short lived. Gold was discovered in 1869, and the gold rush was on. Headlines shouted "Mountains behind San Diego full of gold."

News of this nature tends to travel fast, and soon there was a parade of hopeful men cascading into the gold-filled hills. All means of transportation were employed: oxen, donkeys, horse, and driven men with nothing but packs on their backs. The area soon consisted of fifty tents, some stores, a log cabin, and perhaps more important, at least a dozen saloons.

Julian never became as volatile as some other mining towns, but it did its best to keep up with those who were. There was no doubt that the men were fond of their firewater. On a good Sunday, it was not unusual to have at least twelve decent fights. "Forty rod whiskey" went for ten cents a shot, and some of the men were known to spend a good part of their gold earnings on drink. A vigilante group was formed to help keep outlaws in line. Thankfully, shootouts were rare. Still, the only cemetery in town had what came to be known as "whiskey row," reserved for those gunmen who weren't lucky enough to dodge the bullets.

There were no typical dance halls in Julian, and gambling was kept to a minimum. However, weekly dances kept the miners entertained and a parade of characters provided local color.

One man in particular that piqued the miners' imagination was a fellow known as "Arkensaw." He was a tough mountain man and was afraid of nothing. The rugged gold rush town fit his personality to perfection. No one was more surprised than he when he began to be afraid in his own house. He would awaken in a cold sweat to the sounds of someone groaning in misery. More disturbing was the sound of a razor being sharpened on a leather strap. It would sound faint at first, then intensify to the point where "Arkensaw" would awaken with his heart in his throat, fully expecting to see a madman standing over him with a gleaming weapon. Finally he could stand it no longer and moved to another area. Years afterward miners entertained themselves passing by his house to see where the rough mountain man fell prey to the supernatural.

Gold production reached its peak aout 1874. There were more than two hundred houses in town by this time, most of them not haunted, and strikes were being made in neighboring areas. For a while, the size of the town rivaled San Diego. However, by the mid1900s, large strikes were being made in places like Tombstone, Arizona. Julian's heyday as a gold rush town was over.

Julian soon discovered gold in another form: apples. The area had always been an agricultural paradise. During the gold rush two enterprising businessmen capitalized on this. They began to grow trees that would be well suited to the mountain climate. By the time the gold rush was over, the hillsides were filled with lovely apple trees. This set the stage for what is now one of Julian's main attractions.

Julian is one of San Diego's favorite destinations for a Sunday drive, especially in the fall. Visiting the tiny mountain community is taking a step back to a bygone era. The town has kept its gold rush atmosphere and has made its apple orchards into a profitable tourist trade. People flock there to smell the crisp fall air, shop in the quaint shops, and, of course, indulge in the best apple pie and cider they have ever tasted.

Julian is also a wonderful place to visit at other times of the year. This is expressed beautifully in a poem by Sadie M. Thomas.

Spring greets with wind and flowers;
Summer's heat refreshed by showers;
Golden Autumn with colors glow;
Winter with softly falling snow...
In Julian.

Whatever time of year you choose to visit, you will find Julian a hidden treasure. You may even want to spend the night in the charming Julian Hotel. If you do, by all means request room No. 10. It is Albert Robinson's old room...and he has never left.

*   *   *

The Julian Hotel is a landmark in a town known

for its sense of history. To enter its lobby is to take a step back in time. The rooms have been carefully decorated to capture the feeling of the old gold rush days. Guests and staff alike agree, however, that there is something out of the ordinary about room No. 10.

We know from history that this is the room that Albert occupied when he was alive, and many feel that he has never left. More than one maid has made up the bed, gone to clean the bathroom, only to find the bed messed up again when she returned. Other maids have reported smelling pipe smoke, and one even saw some smoke behind her when she was cleaning a mirror. Most of them are used to this type of activity and share a good attitude about this most unusual guest, telling him that no smoking is allowed.

One guest told of the time when she felt an odd sensation she could not explain. She then saw an image appear before her eyes. It looked like a person without any definite features and it remained for at least two minutes.

Albert is very particular about his room and he does not like anyone to make any changes. Once the owners moved some furniture around in an effort to redecorate. They later returned to find everyhing back the way it was.

It's good to see that a spirit can have a playful side. Albert sometimes hides things from the guests and is fond of slamming doors. The ghost that haunts this lovely hotel was not always so innocent however. There used to be an evil force that possessed the building before it became the Julian Hotel. Great balls of fire could be seen shooting through the rooms. Glass would shatter and furniture would fly across the room on its own. Rumor has it that the citizens grew so concerned that they called an exorcist in to rid the building of the vicious force. Evidently the exorcist succeeded becaus terror no longer reins. Once the Julian Hotel opened, it would seem, Albert made himself right at home.

Albert is by no means confined to his room. He has the run of the entire hotel. Many people are aware of footsteps coming down from the second floor. They look up, expecting to see someone, but no one is there.

There is a beautiful stained glass window that divides the stairs from the dining room. One time the owners knew they were alone in the building, when they heard footsteps and saw a shadow in the window. They investigated, but found no one.

One young couple got into town around nightfall and started to explore the grounds out of curiosity about the historic building. Peering in the window they saw a menu being studied in anticipation for dinner. They were startled to discover no one was holding the menu up. They  walked by later to notice the lacy curtains being pulled apart as if someon was looking out. No doubt that was Room No. 10, and Albert looking over the grounds of his hotel.

The town of Julian is worth a visit from San Diego to experience another era. A walk through town in the crisp mountainair will prepare you for a big slice of warm apple pie in one of the coffee shops. If possible, plan to spend the night. The Julian Hotel is the only one in town and it is an experience in itself. It is a bed and breakfast inn that will take your breath away with its antique furniture, woodburning stove in the lobby, and warm hospitality missing from modern city hotels. It is not hard to see why Albert refuses to leave.

The Julian Hotel
2032 Main Street
Julian
See map, page 94.

Bancroft
Ranch House

The Bancroft Ranch House
A Pretty Ghoul is like a melody, and the melody lingers on.

The August moon sat heavy in the warm summer night sky. The air was filled with the perfume of the season and the sounds of late summer were everywhere. Birds and crickets chirped merrily. Ancient springs gurlgled gently under the ground. The young Indian maiden sat smiling, grinding corn kernels into her matate to make meal for breakfast the next morning. Children of the village laughed and played around her. She sang Indian folksongs softly to herself, for her heart was filled with happiness. She loved this place, just as others had, hundreds of years before her. But her joy was not to last.

Spanish settlers were to push her people from this sacred land that they loved so. As she was led from her home, the tears ran down her beautifully sculpted golden cheeks. She vowed that one day she would return to this magical place with the bubbling waters. Over one hundred years have passed, and the young Indian maiden is at long last back where she belongs.

*   *   *

Over a thousand years of history exists in the area of Spring Valley. At one point about 7,000 Indians occupied the huge Bancroft Ranch region. They were known as the Kamia tribe, and instead of being hunters and gatherers who roamed areas looking for food, these Indians had a permanent community.

They named their community "Neti." One of the reasons for the success of their village was that it sat atop a large underground fresh water spring that was rich in minerals. The Kamia felt the spring was sacred. It was the center of their territory for centuries.

As time went on and the area became more populated with settlers, the Indians began to feel boxed in. They felt their freedom being threatened. The situation came to a head in 1801 when a battle of possession took place between the Spanish, Mexicans, and Indians. Needless to say, the Indians lost, and the victorious Spanish laid claim to all of them. Most were driven out of the area, and a few were made to work in the fields. When the Indians were forced to leave their beloved land, they broke all of their pottery so the Spanish could not use it. By the 1830s, the land was vacant.

A San Diego lawyer claimed part of the ranch in the early 1860s and built the first structure ever constructed there by a white man. It was a two-room adobe, with its frame built with wood obtained from a wrecked sailing ship. It is the same building that stands today.

The most famous person to settle at the ranch was the noted historian, Hubert Howe Bancroft. Bancroft was a well known book publisher from San Francisco who settled in Spring Valley because of its rural atmosphere and mild climate.

Much of what we know about early California history is credited to Bancroft. He wrote historical accounts about Alaska, Canada, Central America, Mexico, and California, a total of thirty-nine in all. He would write eleven to twelve hours a day, standing up all the while. At one time, he donated $100,000 to the

University of California at Berkeley. Today the Berkeley library is named after him and contains all of his works.

When he resided at the ranch, he immersed himself in ranch life. Using many of the Indians still living in the area, he experimented with growing different kinds of fruits and flowers. He lived in the house from 1885 to 1918.

Today the Bancroft Ranch House is operated by the Spring Valley Historical Society, and is used as a place to store relics of the area as well as a reminder of the past. It became an Historical Monument in 1964.

Because its recorded history goes back so far, it is an important part of California history. The house is located near the original Indian burial ground and is invaluable for students of archaeology. San Diego State University students have uncovered countless pieces of pottery and arrowheads. Some of these artifacts are as much as 10,000 years old. They are now displayed in the ranch house museum. The students, as well as other people, have discovered another fascinating fact about this unusual area, some of the original occupants have never left!

*　　　　　*　　　　　*

It's never a good idea to make a public announcement that you don't believe in ghosts. Especially around the Bancroft Ranch House. One of them might hear you. That seems to be what happened to a caretaker at the historic site a number of years ago. Early one morning he was leading a group of Girl Scouts through the house and he thought he would make light of the ghost stories that surround the area, to entertain the girls. He assured them they were only make-believe. He thought nothing of the incident when he returned that evening to lock up. He had been in the artifact room hundreds of times and never found it the least bit frightening. Until that night. In an instant, the door slammed shut and trapped him in the room. He tried in vain to open the door, but it wouldn't move. As he pushed and pulled, beads of sweat rolled down his face until he was drenched in dampness. He never realized how musty and overpowering this room could be. He felt that all the air was being drained from the room, and he was having trouble breathing. He knew his frantic calls for help were unheard as he was the only one on the premises. As he was about to give up all hope, the door suddenly opened. He reached around to find the door was locked from the outside. He knew for a fact no other person was on the grounds. Relieved but shaken, he vowed he would never say he didn't believe in ghosts again.

This is not the only account of strange occurrences in and around the ranch house. Many times the sweet sound of an Indian ballad can be heard drifting on the wind through the trees surrounding the area. Some people tell of seeing a young maiden strolling through the landscape in the moonlight, her long black hair forming a shawl around her shoulders. She is usually humming softly.

Once, on a winter night, one of the caretakers saw a young girl roaming in the mist, singing. She seemed disoriented and the man went over to help her. She drifted away in front of him.

One visitor was interested in metaphysics. She had heard of the legends surrounding the ranch house and decided to do some tests. She walked outside, among the trees, enjoying a quiet evening with a friend. She asked the spirits to give her some sign of their existence. The two friends waited in the still of the quiet night. They repeated the request, but nothing out of the ordinary happened. A little relieved, they laughed sheepishly as they started to walk back to the house. As they got up to leave, a giant eucalyptus tree plunged to the ground, missing them by inches. They had no warning that the tree might fall and the only sound they heard was a loud crack that pierced the night air. Needless to say, this made believers of them both.

Another ghost said to haunt the area is another Indian woman, but this one is nothing like the gentle singing maiden. She is an old lady, in ragged clothes, with tangled black hair that reaches down to her knees. A scowl is visible on her unfriendly face. She appears for an instant, then disappears into oblivion. She has startled many a visitor.

A number of San Diego State University students will never forget their visit to the Bancroft Ranch House. They were archealogy students, there for the night, on an assignment for their class. A number of them saw the aged Indian lady rise up out of the mist that had settled over the grounds. She stood there for a minute, then turned and disappeared into the haze. A few of the students were so unsettled by the experience they ran screming into the night. Two students dropped the class the next day and never returned again. The braver souls did some research and discovered that an Indian Chief's daughter had been cremated on the very spot where the lady had arisen in the mist.

Many people enjoy going to Spring Valley because of its rural atmosphere. The air is fresh and people take life at a slower pace than in the larger city. It is only a fifteen mile drive from downtown San Diego. The Bancroft Ranch House is a treasure for anyone who enjoys looking at artifacts from the past. As you stroll the grounds, you can get a real sense of the people that lived there so many years ago. And if you're lucky, you may even come face to face with one!

Bancroft Ranch House
95 Memory Lane
Spring Valley
Friday, Saturday, Sunday: 1:00 p.m. - 4:00 p.m.
Times and days subject to change.
See map, page 94.

Vallecitos

The Vallecitos Stage Stop
Her vow during life:
Till death do us part.
Her vow during death:
I will not depart.

The sun gleamed brightly off the desert floor as a breeze drifted through the grey-green plants. In the summer the heat would have been unbearable. But this was November. It was crisp, cool, and inviting. The day was perfect for an outdoor wedding. The bride's smile was as bright as the sun as she approached her intended. Her gown was out of a storybook, the delicate fabric shimmering in the desert sun. In the breeze, her lace veil enveloped her in softness. As the couple exchanged their vows, the scene took on a surrealistic quality. It was like a beautiful oasis in the desert.

Later, on an anniversary of that same night, in the moonlight, another young woman in a bridal gown now stands, facing the glowing mountains. This time the bride-to-be has no joy in her heart. She expresses only sadness for her wedding that never took place over one hundred years ago.

*   *   *

The Vallecitos Stage Station has its roots in a long and sometimes violent history. Indians traveled the trail through time immortal. It is even mentioned by a settler that came over on the Spanish Galleon in 1769. The trail became the first mail route between Arizona and California in 1826. The campground was host to a variety of people through the years, including the famed gunslinger Kit Carson. When Julian had its gold rush in the mid-1800s, hopeful prospectors used the campground as a stopover on their way to find their fortunes.

What put the Vallecitos station on the map, however, was the colorful Butterield Stage Line. John Butterfield was awarded a contract by the postmaster general to carry mail and passengers from St. Louis to San Francisco in 1857. He was to organize a group that would build stations, acquire stages, and plot a suitable route for the 2,640-mile trip. It was ready to roll within the year he was allotted to complete the job.

The contract called for them to take the trip twice a week, and they were allotted twenty-five days for the journey. They boasted they could accomplish the feat in twenty-three days, twenty-three hours, and thirty minutes. In those days this was a small marvel.

Vallecitos was one in 165 stations that dotted the line. It became one of the most famous. An unfortunate by-product of the Butterfield Stages was that they attracted bandits like a magnet. Countless times a band of outlaws would await in the bushes, ready to ambush the stage as it went by. The stages did not carry very large amounts of money, but what they did have the bandits were more than happy to take. Vallecitos was not a stranger to the shoot-outs that went along with this kind of lawlessness. A cemetery, still there today, is rumored to be full of bandits who were not clever enough to outsmart the stage drivers.

The Butterfield Stage ran from 1858 to 1861, when the outbreak of the Civil War put an end to the southern part of the line. Various people used the station after this, including Union troops. But after the colorful stageline was discontinued, the station began to crumble. In time it sat in ruins, a faded reminder of California's past.

In 1934 a local civic minded couple showed an interest in restoring the Vallecitos Station. They researched a plan to recreate the historical landmark to its original state of operation. The state approved a grant for the project. Workers were hired, and soon a six-acre state park and campground paid tribute to the Butterfield Stage Line, an institution that was such a part of California's old west.

Today, although about eighty miles out of the city of San Diego, it is a popular area for history buffs as well as campers. It can be easily part of a Sunday drive through the charming mining town of Julian. Because of its proximity to the Anza Borrego State Park, it makes a nice addition to a spring day, when people go to see the wild flowers in all their glory. It is a beautiful, quiet place to contemplate the unique beauty of the desert while enjoying various campground activities. It is also the perfect place on a magical moonlit evening to view the beautiful ghost bride who roams the desert floor, searching for the love that she was denied in her lifetime.

*   *   *

The overland stage coach rides across the country could be rough and they took their toll on more than a few people that could afford the trip. This was especially true of one frail young woman who was never lucky enough to see the end of her journey. She was on her way west to be married, when she grew gravely ill. She made it as far as the Vallecitos stop. She could go on no longer. Knowing that the end was near, she pleaded with the other passengers to please, when the time came, bury her in her wedding dress. She died at the stage station and the people carried out her last wish. She was laid to rest in an unmarked grave.

But that is far from the end of a tragic tale. Throughout the years, stories have been reported of the sighting of a young woman, floating effortlessly over the desert floor in a beautiful white gown.

The vision has become legendary over the years. She is sometimes seen riding a headless black horse, racing relentlessly past the building where she passed from this lifetime. Some people hear the thud of racing hoofbeats. Others actually see the apparition go by, then disappear into another dimension.

When the building was being restored in the 1930s, a new wave of interest arose concerning the ghost bride. Some of the workers who camped there all night felt an uncomfortable presence among them. Because none of them wanted to appear foolish, they kept their feelings to themselves. But finally, the pressure became too much for one of the workmen. He had seen the ghost bride for himself and it was such an unsettling experience he had to quit and find work elsewhere. Hopefully, where people didn't vanish before his eyes.

Today people camping in the area are likely to see her drifting on early evening desert breezes searching in vain for her groom. She sometimes makes an appearance when the weather is not so kind. In the desert there is a weather condition known as the wall cloud. It comes out of the northwest and portends high winds and twisters, especially in the spring. This possibility of a violent climate seems to stir the turbulence within her soul. It is thought that a wall cloud had gathered on the day she died.

The area is rich with other tales of strange occurrences. A well known one is that of the phantom stage. The drivers of the Butterfield Stage usually had a guard accompany them on their journeys. On this fateful night, the driver's guard took ill and had to be left behind. In order to keep on schedule, the brave driver had to cross the desert alone, in the inky blackness, with only a sliver of a moon to guide him. Just as he was relieved to see the Vallecitos Station in the distance, a bandit attacked, robbed and killed him at point blank range. The frightened horses galloped away, with the stage still attached.

Old prospectors often saw the phantom stage approach in the dead of night. They heard the creaking, the wheels turning in the sand, and the sounds of the horses. The stage appeared to them for an instant, and then vanished.

Today campers, most unaware of the legend, report to park officials they are sure they heard the sound of a stage pulled by horses approach the campground. They usually think they were dreaming, until they find fresh wagon tracks and ruts around the camp in the morning.

Another story involves a white horse. A band of outlaws robbed a stage and got in a shoot-out near the Vallecitos Station. The leader of the pack, on a magnificent white horse, and one other bandit were the sole survivors. They had stolen an unusually large amount of money from this stage and decided to bury it before going on. After arriving at the station, the leader thought twice about sharing the loot with his partner in crime. He burst into the station on his white horse to have it out with the other bandit. In the battle both were killed, and the white horse ran away.

People have been treasure hunting in the desert ever since that story was made public. Legend has it if you get anywhere near the buried treasure, you'll hear the pounding of horses' hooves and see a large white horse appear out of nowhere. By this time people get a little intimidated and lose interest. So far as it is known, the gold is still somewhere out there. But so is the large white horse, ready to protect its treasure.

A related story involves an illuminated skeleton. It is thought that it might belong to the man on the

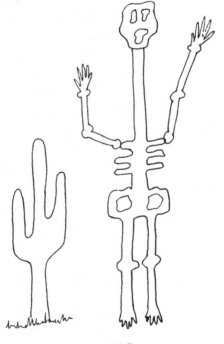

white horse. One prospector awoke one night when his burros began getting restless. He saw the image of a skeleton with a faint glow coming from its rib cage. He told other prospectors about how the sight got his "bones a-rattlin'." He was not the only one to see the strange image. Two other prospectors had the same chilling experience. Since those early times, the skeleton has been sighted again and again. Apparently it isn't mere mortals who are set on finding the treasure buried somewhere in the Vallecitos area.

It is not hard to understand why there are so many varied ghost stories in the desert. Its past is one of love lost, violence and treachery. It stands to reason her legends would be as lively as her history.

The drive to Vallecitos is a beautiful one. It is reached by taking highway 78 east to S-2, also known as the Great Southern Overland Stage Route. Go up through Scissors Crossing and down onto the desert floor. Pass by the Box Canyon historical area, the Cain Valley rock formations, and beautiful desert plants. You'll see Spanish Moss growing on some of the vegetation. It seems to glow in the sun. When you spot the Butterfield Stage Cafe you are only about five miles from your destination.

There is a monument that gives a short history of the stageline. There are picnic tables and camping facilities. There is an authentic recreation of the stage station, looking much like it did on a devastating day many years ago when a young woman lost her life. There is also a feeling of excitement and anticipation. For you never know, in this strange land known as the desert, just which one of the cast of characters Vallecitos has to offer will make contact with you tonight

See map, page 94.

Point Loma Lighthouse

Point Loma Lighthouse

The Lighthouse Keeper
Still Keeps House!

The red and white flashing of the lighthouse lantern hypnotized the crusty keeper on watch in the glass enclosure. Even with the sound of the wind outside it lulled him into a quiet warmth and sense of well being. It was a stark contrast to the blustery turmoil taking place just outside his safe haven. Southern California, he thought. Sunny skies, calm beaches, gentle breezes drifting through the palms. Suddenly, he heard the familiar sound of the ships' foghorns calling for help from the turbulent sea below. He took the spiral steps down by twos as he ran to help them. Before he left the lighthouse he grabbed his shotgun he always left in the corner by the door. With the wind howling around him he ran to the cliff's edge and fired three loud shots into the air. Then three more. The bright red and white light pierced the darkness like a colorful knife above his head. Below, a blanket of fog covered the sea like soft cotton clouds. Three more shots rang out. He finally saw the ships' masts slowly turn away from the rocky cliffs below. They were safe. This time...

* * *

The lure of the California gold rush brought with it a parade of characters hoping to make their fortune in the Golden State. Merchants, settlers, and prospectors all needed a beacon to guide them to the riches on the West Coast. In the mid-1800s Congress proposed that eight lighthouses be built along the California shore.

San Diego's Point Loma became the home of one of the first of them. The site, high above the beautiful protected harbor, was perfect for such an undertaking. However, at this time in our young history, San Diego's main community, Old Town, was still just a village. The lack of roads, people, and drinking water made the building of the lighthouse a difficult project. There were also endless administrative problems. Yes, red tape was alive and well even in the past!

In 1854 the Point Loma lighthouse became a working site. Once built, there was the problem of keeping the keepers happy. Low pay and the lonely life style kept many people away. The assistants were paid even less, and sometimes kept twenty-four hour watches. In nineteen years the lighthouse saw ten different keepers. It also suffered many different political and operating problems.

In 1871, the lighthouse's most well known keeper, Captain Robert D. Israel, became the assistant. Two years later he became the permanent keeper of the flame. He was born on the East Coast and heroically served in the Mexican American War. After the war he moved to San Diego, where he became an active member of the small but growing community. He married into a prominent family by taking for his bride the granddaughter of one of the founding settlers of San Diego, the Machado family. His bride was Maria Archdia Alipas.

For twenty years the Israel family lovingly tended to the workings of the Point Loma lighthouse. They raised four sons while there. Because of their growing family, a near-by home was built for them. It was a solitary existence, but they took joy in the company of their family. Supplies were brought in quarterly and would include books and plants that would support a small garden. Mrs. Israel especially took pride in her tomato vines. In fact Mrs. Israel was the assistant lighthouse keeper for three years, helping her husband keep watch over the sea below. She would spend much of her lookout time knitting in the glow of the lighthouse lantern. Robert Israel took pride in the fact that there were so few accidents on the rocky cliffs below. He became well known for firing his shot gun high into the night sky to warn wayward ships that they were getting too close to the coast. Many times the fog would shield their view of the flashing red and white beacon above.

In 1891 the lighthouse was abandoned. A new one went into operation at a location at the water's edge where the approaching ships could finally see the warning light below the fog line. The Israel family moved there for a while, but again ran into administrative problems. After a pay cut, they decided they had had enough of lighthouse keeping, and moved to Coronado, across the bay. Captain Israel died in the year 1908.

For forty years the lighthouse stood abandoned. In 1913 President Woodrow Wilson declared the lighthouse a national monument. However, nothing of significance was done to restore the aging building. It attracted visitors who loved to climb the tower to take in the magnificent view. Unfortunately, it also attracted its share of vandals. It looked like the life of the old Point Loma lighthouse had come to an end.

Around this same time a movement was underway to erect a monument to Juan Rodriquez Cabrillo, the man who discovered the West Coast of the United States in 1542. A one-half acre plot surrounding the lighthouse was purchased, and the lighthouse was saved, becoming part of the Cabrillo National Monument! The monument was turned over to the National Park Service in 1933 and work was begun to restore the lighthouse to its original condition. They took special care to make sure it looked like it did when the proud Captain Israel stepped out to tend to his chores. Some of the furnishings are even the original belongings of the Israel family.

The Cabrillo National Monument is one of the most visited state parks in the country. It has one of the most beautiful views in the world. People use the site to watch the mighty gray whales on their annual migration. They visit the museum to learn of the discovery of the western United States. They can climb the old lighthouse stairs to look for ships much like the keepers did so many years ago. Today the lighthouse is alive!!! IT EVEN HAS A GHOST....

*　　　　　　*　　　　　　*

Rumors have existed for years about the ghost that haunts the old Point Loma lighthouse. It's easy to see why. Even on a sunny, picture perfect 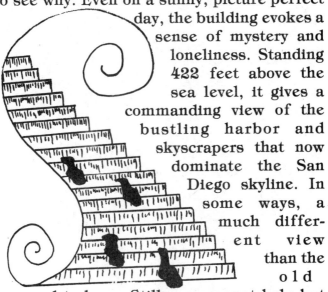 day, the building evokes a sense of mystery and loneliness. Standing 422 feet above the sea level, it gives a commanding view of the bustling harbor and skyscrapers that now dominate the San Diego skyline. In some ways, a much differ-ent view than the o l d keepers used to have. Still, one cannot help but feel they are looking into the past....

Who is the ghost that dominates the mood of this special place? Many think it is Captain Israel himself! Too many odd things occur to count out the fact that the old captain still considers this point of land to be his turf. Museum workers will tell you that the alarm installed for security reasons has recently gone off in the late night hours. Knowing something had to set it off, the of-ficials turn up expecting to find some vandals at work. They find no one. Or at least no one they can see!

If you make the climb to the top of the tower, you can be sure to feel the cool sea breeze brush across your face. But, like others, you may also feel the equally cool stare of an unknown presence that is perhaps not too happy about someone else treading on his domain. Standing on the cliff's edge, sometimes a loud shattering sound can be heard. The beginnings of a storm? Maybe. Or it could be the sound of Captain Israel's infamous shotgun warning ships of impending danger.

The homey smell of freshly baked bread can be detected along with the salty sea air from an oven that has long ago stopped working. Once in a while, the gentle sound of a rocking chair and knitting needles can be heard from the first floor of the lighthouse building where Mrs. Israel diligently worked on her homemade projects for her family.

And finally — don't be surprised, when peering out to sea on a foggy night, to see swirls of red mixed in with the down whiteness of the fog. Captain Israel's light still shines to provide a very special link to San Diego's past.

Point Loma Lighthouse
Cabrillo Monument
Located at the south end of Catalina Boulevard, Point Loma.
9:00-6:15 - Summer through Labor Day.
9:00-5:15 - Winter hours.

124